Ancient Peoples and Places

SOUTH EAST ENGLAND

General Editor

DR GLYN DANIEL

ABOUT THE AUTHOR

Ronald Jessup, a well-known Fellow of the Society of Antiquaries, was born in Kent where for three generations his family had connections with the lime and cement trade. From an early age he was familiar with the flint implements and antiquities in his grandfather's collection and can remember the tricks of the quarrymen in foisting their home-made antiquities upon voracious collectors. He has written several books and many papers on various aspects of archaeology and was the first archaeologist in Britain to make his own film-strips as a day-to-day record of excavations. Ronald Jessup's particular interest is in the Roman burial-mounds and walled cemeteries of Europe, for a study of which he was given the Taylor Medal of the British Archaeological Association and an Award by the Leverhulme Foundation.

SOUTH EAST ENGLAND

Ronald Jessup

75 PHOTOGRAPHS
57 LINE DRAWINGS
2 MAPS
1 CHART

 THAMES AND HUDSON

THIS IS VOLUME SIXTY-NINE IN THE SERIES

Ancient Peoples and Places

GENERAL EDITOR: DR GLYN DANIEL

CONTENTS

ILLUSTRATIONS

8

W. N. : In Happy Memory

Foreword

TO CONFORM WITH an over-all plan the present volume is concerned with the counties of Kent, Surrey and Sussex. The series already includes East Anglia, Wessex and South West England to which it is hoped the Thames Basin and the Southern Midlands may be added. The deliberate length of Chapter 8 is a measure of the extent of Roman studies during recent years. The departure of the Romans has been chosen to mark the end of the book but the story of ancient peoples and places in the south-east of England continued, of course, with vigour and determination.

I have had the great advantage of being able to discuss certain aspects of this book with my brother, Frank W. Jessup, with Dr John Alexander, Professor B. W. Cunliffe, Professor Christopher Hawkes, Miss Joan Liversidge, Professor Stuart Piggott, Mr T. G. E. Powell and with the Editor, Dr Glyn Daniel. To them all I am indeed grateful, but it must not be assumed that they necessarily agree with what I have said. Messrs J. H. Evans, L. R. Allen Grove, D. B. Kelly, Colonel G. W. Meates and Mr P. J. Tester of the Kent Archaeological Society, Messrs A. W. G. Lowther, E. E. Harrison and E. S. Wood of the Surrey Archaeological Society, and Messrs G. A. Holleyman, J. H. Money, N. E. S. Norris and Dr F. W. Steer of the Sussex Archaeological Society have kindly advised me on matters in which they have specialized knowledge. Many individuals and organizations have been most generous in allowing me to use illustrations; they are noted in detail later in the book.

R. J.

CHAPTER I

The Topographical Background

KENT, SURREY and Sussex constitute a clearly defined natural area, with striking physical features common to the three counties and, except for the main chalk hills, scarcely extending beyond their borders. The area is some 100 miles long and 50 miles broad. Its western boundary is the Hampshire basin, the northern the river Thames with its wide estuary and seaward waters, while on the south and the east lie the English Channel and the Strait of Dover. From the chalk mass of Hampshire two ridges run eastward across the area, one forming the South Downs and reaching the sea at Beachy Head, the other forming the longer range of the North Downs and terminating in the chalk headland of the South Foreland on the Strait of Dover. Between these two ridges and half enclosed by them lies the Weald, practically the whole of which is within the three counties of Kent, Surrey and Sussex. The country lying to the north of the North Downs forms part of the London basin; south of the South Downs part of the coasts of Kent and Sussex are covered by alluvial marsh.

Fig. 1

The White Cliffs of Dover are but twenty-one miles from the long line of chalk hills of the Bas Boulonnais coast. The chalk hills of East Kent of which they are the bastion, and the Thames, facing the Scheldt and Rhine—the great European rivers which from earliest times have been highroads of folk-movement, ideas, trade and civilization—have long been the principal approaches to the British Isles. To them came both refugee and conqueror. They came not only across the Narrow Seas. The Channel also provided access to the coasts of Sussex and Kent by way of an Atlantic route along which Iberia, Brittany and Cornwall were ultimate and intermediate stopping-places. The large peninsula of the south-east was in prehistory as well as in history the gateway of England. There were also landward approaches from the west. The chalk downs and the upper reaches of the Thames gave access to the prehistoric centre of north-western Europe in Wessex and in the Bronze Age, for example, indirectly to sources of Irish gold. In view of its geographical situation the south-east was open to the fertilization and cross-fertilization of almost every influence that the sea might bring. Its natural advantages of situation and generally fertile soils also gave every encouragement to native tradition and development.

THE DOWNS

The dominant physical features are the chalk ridges of the North and South Downs. In Kent the summit of the North Downs is rarely less than 600 feet above sea level; it rises to nearly 900 feet on the escarpment above Oxted in Surrey just beyond the boundary of Kent but falls considerably from that height between Guildford and Farnham where the great angle of dip results in the Hog's Back, a narrow ridge only a few hundred feet broad at the top. The South Downs rise to 837 feet at Duncton and to just over 800 feet at Ditching Beacon, scarcely the 'chain of majestic mountains' described by Gilbert White; but these gently swelling rolling hills at their finest between Ditchling Beacon and Beachy Head and in the sweeping downs that culminate in Firle Beacon, especially when they are viewed from the north, perhaps made on early man something of the very strong and enduring impression that they leave on the traveller of the present day.

Plate 1

The Downs are the projecting remnants of a vast dome of chalk covered with sedimentary deposits and underlaid by older wealden rocks, much cracked at the remote geological time of their elevation by a vast compression in Alpine regions and subsequently worn down to their present form by the natural agencies of river-action, frost, wind and rain. Steep scarps slope inwards towards the Weald, a concentric series of much weathered beds of older, less resistant clays and sandstone rocks once underlying

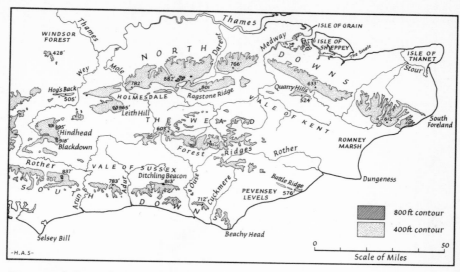

Fig. 1   Relief map of south-east England

the chalk dome, and there is a broad and for the most part gentle dip-slope often intersected by dry valleys northward to the Thames and southward to the Channel. Apart from areas on the summits covered locally by the superficial clay-with-flints, an in-tractable soil, the well-drained dip-slope with light loamy and intermediate soils found favour from Neolithic to Roman times and later. But it is only on the lower slopes away from the escarp-ment as on the east side of the Elham Valley and in the Isle of Thanet in East Kent, and the country by Sutton and Epsom in Surrey, that the North Downs are, like the South Downs, wholly free from these superficial deposits. The consistent settlement of the South Downs during Neolithic and Bronze Age times is a reflection of the more favourable soil conditions. In both regions water-supply must have been a major problem as it still is at the present time, a problem alleviated however by the damp climate and perhaps by the use of dew-ponds on the South Downs though they seem never to have been constructed in the northern chalk country where the intermittent springs sometimes rose in dry valleys cut low enough to reach the then higher water-table of the chalk.

The Downs maintain an average height of 500–700 feet, and there is a steep fall of some 400 feet to the underlying formations of the Upper Greensand and Gault Clay of the Weald. River gaps through the chalk ridges have inevitably had great influence on the nature and pattern of human settlement. Along the North Downs the principal gaps are the Wey at Guildford, the Mole (Leatherhead-Dorking), the Merstham (now dry) gap (Redhill-Reigate) the Darent (Otford-Farningham), the Med-way (Rochester-Maidstone), and the Kentish Stour (Canterbury-Ashford). Along the South Downs there are gaps carved by the Arun (Arundel), the Adur (Steyning), the Ouse (Lewes) and the Cuckmere west of Beachy Head. Apart perhaps from the very Central Weald, no area in the south-east was far from a waterway, and riverside gravels and loams were obvious attrac-tions for early settlers. The great and sustained importance of river crossings, on the Lower and Middle Thames for example and at Aylesford on the Medway, Crayford on the Darent and in the Stour gap near Canterbury, is evident from the large number and variety of antiquities found there.

In contrast to the many north-south river gaps, the downland country provides the only natural east to west land route. The North-Downs Trackway, ridgeway or terraceway according to the nature of the surface soil in the several seasons and the natural lie of the land, and traditionally associated for lengths of its terraceway course with the Pilgrims' Way, runs from the Dover shore in a long westerly course to Hampshire and by the Harroway to Salisbury Plain and the chalklands of Wessex. By way of the Berkshire Downs and the Chiltern Hills it also provided com-munication with these regions as well as with the Brecklands of East Anglia, all of which were well settled in prehistoric times though not primarily from the south-east. There is an interesting

Plate 2

speculation that in its original course this route may have linked the south-east to the Continent before the final breaching of the Strait of Dover. Direct evidence of its early use is difficult to find; it passes through the Iron Age hill-fort at Bigbury, Kent. Belgic coins have been discovered along its course, and in Kent and Surrey parts of the route were used in Roman times. Along the South Downs local ridgeways form ways of communication between the causewayed enclosures of the Neolithic cattle breeders.

Until the Second World War most of the downland remained open and unenclosed with its prehistoric and Roman sites visible and generally accessible. Intensive ploughing then led to the destruction and damage of many sites, although a large number had fortunately been studied and properly recorded, and there is now much less freedom of access.

THE WEALD

The centre of the south-eastern area and its oldest exposed rock formation is the high Forest Ridges of the Weald extending from near Horsham to the sea near Hastings. This region of sands and clays underlying the chalk reaches its highest point, just over 790 feet, near Crowborough and on its hills lie the heathy wastes of St Leonard's, Tilgate and Ashdown Forests which formed the heart of the forest of Anderida, the Andredesweald of the Saxons which gave its name to the district. The drier sandy soil of the central Forest Ridge was visited occasionally by Mesolithic hunters, but the tangled heavy woodland and deep clay bottoms long formed a barrier against invasion and movement; the forested landscape is shown by the prevalence of place-names ending in -*den*, -*hurst*, and -*ley*, and the late settlement by the large size of the parishes and the Domesday record of but eight manors in the whole of the Weald of Kent. In the Iron Age and in Roman times there was exploitation of natural resources for iron-smelting, but both before and immediately after the Roman occupation the High Weald had very little attraction for major human settlement.

The Forest Ridges are surrounded on all sides but the seaward by a much lower area of flat clayland, the Vales of Kent and Sussex. The thick impervious Weald Clay is difficult to drain and its cold wet grassland and infertile soil, once a continuous damp oak forest, was scarcely visited until late in the Early Iron Age when potters made occasional use of the clay and rather later when there was some Roman industry in tile-making and iron-smelting. It was this land that Cobbett in 1823 described as 'the real weald, where the clay is bottomless'. In 1791 it was said to be disgusting to ride over, and most discouraging to farm in. Earlier man left it severely alone.

Forming a rim round almost the whole of the Vale country are the ridges of the Greensand which in their northern development reach a height of 965 feet, considerably higher than the Downs, at Leith Hill in Surrey and a little over 900 feet at Hindhead and Blackdown further westward. The Ragstone Ridge and the Quarry Hills are its outstanding central and eastern features. In no other area in the south-east is there such a wide variation in the soil-mantle as that on the Greensand. In east and mid Kent, it is extremely fertile and easy to work; in the area of its greatest natural development, as between Leith Hill and Guildford, it is open heath-land or covered with woods of fir, larch and birch. Hindhead, near the heart of this region, Cobbett called 'the most villainous spot that God ever made'. But for early prehistoric man who lived by hunting and fishing the Greensand country with good drainage, an abundance of springs and easily traversed light woodland, provided food and shelter under optimum conditions. It found favour also among the tribes of the Early Iron Age, as is exemplified by their hill-forts.

Plate 3

The valley of the Medway between Yalding and Maidstone was well farmed in Roman times and probably earlier, and the Kentish ragstone, quarried on a commercial scale for building purposes, was exported by river-transport to the Roman city of London (Londinium) and by road, far beyond.

From the Greensand ridge the face of the land falls gradually until it reaches the narrow Gault Clay vale which at its western end is known as the Holmesdale. Its stiff but often loamy surface near outcrops of Greensand and Chalk makes a rich and easily cultivated soil which was worked from Neolithic times onwards. Everywhere the vale of the Gault Clay is overlooked by the steep scarp of the Chalk Downs under which it dips.

THE LONDON BASIN

From the top of the North Downs escarpment the land begins to fall away in the gentle slopes of a broad flat plateau towards the Thames and its wide estuary. A great part of the region is occupied by the geologically younger Tertiary sands, pebble beds, clays and loams which rest on the chalk. In the north and north-east with its light and intermediate soils it has always been an extremely fertile country. There are however regions of coarse sand and pebbles such as the still unenclosed commons of Hayes and Blackheath in north-west Kent and the extensive commons and barren heaths in Surrey—Cobbett's country of 'Spewy sand'—that have never been of much use to agriculturists though the heathland habitat supported early forest-culture peoples and later a few pastoralists.

Along the course of the Thames and its tributary streams the spreads and terraces of porous gravel deposited during the long physiographical evolution of their systems supported an easily cleared light woodland suitable for hunting, early settlement and in due course food production and farming. Here also there are large tracts of the fertile loams generically known as brick-earth which were dropped by the rivers in flood, and both here and along the south coast such areas supported settlement from early prehistoric times. Above all, the pattern of prehistoric and early historic settlement was governed by the ease of communication both by water and by land from the largest estuary on the eastern seaboard of Britain.

The physiography of the Thames and its evolution in the Pleistocene period were highly complex. During the three first glaciations, ice-sheets extended as far south as the northern part of its basin, and as a result of the two earliest of these phases the course of the river was diverted from the Vale of St Albans and central Essex to approximately its present course through the site of London. The southern limit of the ice-sheet was roughly along this line, from which melt-waters spread out fans of gravel, sand, clay and brick-earth and high winds from time to time built up deposits of loess in limited areas. Between glaciations the ice disappeared completely for long periods of time, when the climate was as mild as or milder than it is at present. Great changes took place in the relative levels of sea and land. The raised beaches of the

Plate 4

Sussex coast and the various gravel terraces cut by the rivers point to sea-levels well above the present, while a deep channel which was later infilled and completely buried was cut when the sea was far below its present level. It was during the long warm period of the Hoxnian (Second) Interglacial, when the Thames cut its 100-foot terrace, that Man first appeared in the south-east and indeed in Britain.

THE MARSHLANDS

The estuaries of the Thames and Medway, the Wantsum Channel separating the Isle of Thanet from the mainland, and the course of the Kentish Stour, are distinguished by extensive spreads of marshland, and this feature is also to be seen on a much larger scale on the south coast in Romney Marsh and in the Pevensey Levels farther west. Selsey Bill, the most southerly point in the south-east, is the remaining part of a drowned peninsula, more than half of which seems to have disappeared within historical times. Most of the marshlands have been reclaimed from the sea in comparatively recent times, but the Rhee Wall, an earthen bank between Appledore and Romney which played an important part in the formation of Romney Marsh, may be late Roman work.

The present area known as Romney Marsh was inhabited in Belgic and early Roman times, and it was not until late in the Roman period that a pronounced rise in sea-level perhaps of as much as 10 feet resulted in widespread inundation. The small marsh-island of Lydd was occupied by a farming and fishing community throughout the Roman period and well into the Dark Ages, and its church may just possibly have started as a Roman basilica.

The present dissected appearance of the Medway marshes, which in Elizabethan times occupied a much larger area, is due to the destruction of protective sea-walls following large-scale commercial excavations for clay and mud which began in the nineteenth century. Many discoveries of prehistoric and Roman antiquities made then and since point to the great changes which have taken place in the relative levels of land and sea and to a long continued subsidence in the south-east. In the Medway marshes, the surface of the land has sunk as much as 15 feet since the first century AD. Unfortunately there is as yet no exact chronology as there is in the Fenland of East Anglia: information to establish the archaeological significance of the subsidence is an outstanding need.

Late Bronze Age gold ornaments and coins of the pre-Roman Iron Age have been found on the shore at Selsey, and here the site of a flourishing Saxon minster has been completely submerged. By way of contrast the great shingle spit of Dungeness on the south coast has been building up for a long period of time, and recent discoveries made far out on Denge Marsh suggest that the process was well established by the second century.

The south-east appears often in the history of British archaeology. Many of its monuments have long been recognized as national antiquities, while the number and variety of discoveries constantly made within the region at least since the days when such matters first attracted attention have assured its place in the literature of archaeology.

The well-known antiquarian topographers of the sixteenth and seventeenth centuries made frequent mention both of sites and of discoveries. Leland, in the liberal interpretation of his royal commission of 1533, looked far beyond the libraries which were his primary concern, and his famous *Itinerary* first published by Hearne in 1710–12 contains, for example, descriptions of the Saxon cross at Reculver, the finding of Roman coins at various places, of a lead coffin in a Roman barrow at Canterbury, and he notes in his description of the Roman fort at Richborough that he 'had antiquities of the heremite, the which is an industrius man'. William Lambarde the Kentish lawyer who in 1576 published his *Perambulation of Kent*, the first of our county histories, used some of Leland's material, but apart from noticing a Roman barrow at Holborough, barrows in Greenwich Park which he thought to be the burial places of fourteenth-century rebels, and giving in a very disinterested way an account of Richborough, he has little to say about antiquities though much about antiquity. Camden also used some of Leland's manuscript material, but he often saw for himself. At Richborough 'draughts of streets crossing one another, for where they have gone the corn is thinner', in his *Britannia*, 1586, is the earliest record of a crop-site. He also described with first-hand knowledge Kits Coty, Julliberrie's Grave and certain dene-holes, and his drawing of the medieval inscription still to be seen at St John's-sub-Castro, Lewes, is the earliest archaeological illustration in an English book. In 1673, John Aubrey began his *Natural History and Antiquities of Surrey* which was not published until 1719. Its five volumes owe much to various editions of Camden, but include some personal observations of antiquities. Surrey also provided the background for an early county archaeology, Nicholas Salmon's valuable and entertaining *Antiquities of Surrey*, 1736, a work not unlike Aubrey's but based rather on observation from a carriage window. An outstanding piece of antiquarian carto-graphy the *Philosophico-Chorographical Chart of East Kent* was published in 1737 by Christopher Packe, a Canterbury doctor. William Stukeley's *Itinerarium Curiosum*, 1725, is of great value for its drawings and plans which include views of barrows and Roman roads, the Chichester inscription, bronze palstaves from Margate and an earthwork near Staines which was lost until it appeared on an air-photograph more than two centuries later. Hasted's *History of Kent*, 1778–98, Manning and Bray's *History of Surrey*, 1804, and T. W. Horsfield's *History, Antiquities and Topography of Sussex*, 1835, with their frequent attention to field monuments and discoveries inaugurate the modern literary scene.

Apart from treasure-hunts under Royal licence, the earliest excavation of which there is record was made in Saxon graves at Chartham, Kent, in 1730, and in the same countryside there followed in 1757–73 the extensive excavation of Saxon graves by a parson-antiquary Bryan Faussett whose remarkable collection is now a chief treasure in the Liverpool City Museums. Faussett was the first to recognize the Anglo-Saxons in their archaeological context. In the 1780's James Douglas, another parson-antiquary and ex-mercenary soldier, was excavating in Kent, Sussex and elsewhere in Britain. He was the first antiquary to produce a plan of a site which he had excavated, again a Saxon barrow, and his *Nenia Britannica*, 1793, contains much direct field observation amid its curious fancies. In 1785, Douglas read to the Royal Society a *Dissertation on the Antiquity of the Earth* based partly on the evidence of fossils he had obtained from undisturbed sands and gravels of the Medway and, greatly daring, pointed out the true significance of undisturbed geological deposits and chal-lenged the idea of a Universal Deluge in north Kent. His views were received with cold contempt. The formation of county archaeological societies—Sussex in 1846, Surrey in 1854 and Kent in 1857—and the Congress of the newly-formed British

Archaeological Association at Canterbury in 1844 at once encouraged excavation, not all of it by way of a social grace, and
gave to publication a proper status. Famous names in the latter
years of the nineteenth century, among them Pitt Rivers and
Greenwell in Sussex and Arthur Evans at Aylesford in Kent,
placed the south-east firmly in its national archaeological background and indicated something of its continental connections.

CHAPTER II

The Earliest Inhabitants
Hunters and Food-Gatherers

UNTIL A FEW YEARS ago this book would have started with a discussion of eoliths, the battered flints from the high plateau gravels of the North Downs in Kent which were often regarded as among the earliest relics of man's life in Britain. The disputes which they excited, often conducted with bitterness and intense local rivalries, are now part of the history of archaeology and it has been shown statistically and beyond reasonable doubt that the rough chipping and flaking of these 'dawn stones' was produced by natural causes. Benjamin Harrison, the grocer of Ightham who first discovered them and became their leading champion, is commemorated in the village church by a tablet which incorporates an eolith he collected in 1865; a more fitting memorial to his wide out-of-doors interests is the dedication of the megalith at Coldrum, a monument now in the care of the National Trust.

The earliest traces of man in the south-east, as elsewhere in Britain, are in fact the coarse thick flake tools, choppers and cores of the Clactonian industry; these appear in the gravels of the 100-foot terrace of the Lower Thames and in a raised beach in West Sussex. At the base of the Thames gravels, which were laid down in the early part of the Hoxnian Interglacial, the Clactonian implements are distinguished by their smooth surface and a deep chocolate-coloured patina which suggests a derivation from an earlier period, but at a higher level they are more carefully worked and unworn and conform more closely with tools from the type-site, an old channel of the Thames relating to the penultimate glaciation now exposed at Clacton-on-Sea, Essex.

The geological structure of south-eastern England is not in general favourable to the natural formation of caves suited to human habitation. There are no cave-dwellings such as those used at certain seasons by hunters of the Middle and Upper Palaeolithic elsewhere in Britain. Caves in the chalk, in Thanet and at Chislehurst in Kent and near Farnham, Dorking and Guildford in Surrey, have sometimes been claimed as habitations of prehistoric man, but like many of the so-called dene-holes there is no satisfactory evidence of their age and most are likely to be relatively modern quarries for marl and chalk rock. It must also be remembered that the face of the land suffered vast changes during the glacial and interglacial phases of Pleistocene time, and much evidence may have disappeared. Of all the more in-terest therefore are the remains of two rock-shelters (on the east
side of the Iron Age hill fort) on Oldbury Hill, Ightham, Kent, which may well have been used by hunters of the Old Stone Age. One is a natural penthouse formed by the local hard green chert of the Folkestone Beds, the other a shallow cavern in sand hardened by the percolation of water heavily charged with iron salts. Both were much damaged by quarrying operations in the nineteenth century, and natural weathering and the depredations of children from the near-by housing estate in recent years have taken their toll. The suggested prehistoric occupation is based on evidence obtained during excavations made at the foot of the larger shelter in 1890 by the British Association for the Advance-ment of Science at the instigation of Benjamin Harrison. The ex-cavations yielded a series of flint hand-axes worked on both faces, many of them sharp and unabraded, and a large number of waste flakes; among them Mousterian hand-axes and Levallois flakes can be recognized clearly, and it is a fair inference that the tools were made by people who took advantage of shelter afforded by the overhanging rocks. It is known that a cave of some size was

Plate 5

CHART: *The Palaeolithic in south-east England. Dates are approximate and in thousands of years. Sites may overlap in chronology*

Date BC	Climatic Phases	Archaeology							Sites
	POST-GLACIAL			MESOLITHIC					
10	FOURTH GLACIATION								
100	IPSWICH (THIRD) INTERGLACIAL	UPPER PLEISTOCENE			LEVALLOISEAN	MOUSTERIAN	UPPER	PALAEOLITHIC	Thames 50 ft terrace Baker's Hole Crayford Sussex 15 ft raised beach
	THIRD GLACIATION								
300	HOXNE (SECOND OR GREAT) INTERGLACIAL	MIDDLE	CHELLEAN ACHEULIAN	CLACTONIAN					Thames 100 ft terrace Swanscombe Skull Bowman's Lodge Cuxton Sussex 100 ft raised beach Slindon
	SECOND GLACIATION								
500	CROMER (FIRST) INTERGLACIAL	LOWER					LOWER		Fordwich
	FIRST GLACIATION								

also destroyed by stone quarrying, and it is not impossible that others may still exist hidden by a covering of surface soil. Many other implements have been found in the gravels on the lower slopes of the hill.

Although no other physical traces have been preserved, living-places of the hunters and food-gatherers may be inferred from the presence of their flint workshops or working-floors, several of which have come to light in south-eastern England. These we shall now consider before giving some account of the vast numbers of other flint implements and of the skeletal remains of Palaeolithic man himself.

A workshop site of the later Levallois industry discovered at Crayford in the Lower Thames Valley by Flaxman C. J. Spurrell in 1880 is of more than usual interest. Here, under 36 feet of water-deposited brick-earths of the 50-foot terrace, Spurrell, an accurate field-worker the full value of whose important and well-recorded researches in North Kent were not apparent until they could be set against modern appreciations of geology and archaeology, found the lower jaw of a woolly rhinoceros lying on a pile of flint flakes with one flake firmly cemented to the jaw. It seems likely that the animal formed part of the flint-worker's food supply. There were many flake-tools and blades, and Spurrell collected all the tortoise-cores, chips and flakes with assiduity. From more than sixty flakes which he assembled round one core he was able to reconstruct the original flint nodule almost completely. The bones of the woolly rhinoceros and of other cold-loving animals found in the brick-earth indicate a change from warmer southern conditions to a period of increasing cold, and it is possible that in times of inclement weather the Crayford workshop people had to abandon an open-air life and retreat to a chalk cave. An equally interesting but perhaps earlier Levallois industry came to light in 1911 in a chalk-quarry known as Baker's Hole at Northfleet six miles east of Crayford. The site has long been quarried away, but there seems to be no

Fig. 2

Fig. 2 Baker's Hole, North-fleet, Kent. Tortoise core. Length 6.5 ins

Fig. 3 Baker's Hole, Northfleet, Kent. Levallois flake-tool struck from tortoise core. Length 7 ins

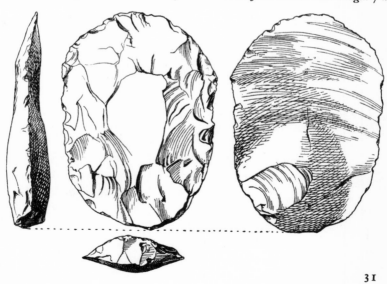

31

Fig. 3

doubt that it was related to the 50-foot terrace of the Thames although it was situated by the side of the Ebbsfleet, a small stream emptying into the Thames at Northfleet. A few tools came from the terrace gravels, but hundreds of large oval tortoise-cores, triangular and heart-shaped hand-axes, and flakes with faceted striking-platforms, some of them quite thin, had been inundated by Coombe Rock from the neighbouring hillside. The number of mis-struck tools and flakes reflects the difficulties of the Levallois technique. The sludge deposit, whatever its precise geological age, showed evidence of great and rapid movement—and in places it was later removed down to the surface of the underlying chalk—and in its advance must have wrought great destruction, not only to the flint workshop but also to human and animal life. It should be said, however, that the human skull to be noticed later which was apparently found above the level of the floor is most unlikely to be the remains of one of the flint-workers. The Crayford and Northfleet flints, most of which are in the British Museum and the British Museum (Natural History), remain as the best known examples of the Levallois industry in Britain. The geological significance of this deposit of Coombe Rock is now difficult to assess as no satisfactory exposures are available for study. It seems to belong to one of the two phases of the Penultimate (Third) Glaciation, but it could be argued, and the flint industry shows similarities to the Levallois stage V of the Somme, that it was a result of frost soil-weathering during the Last (Fourth) Glaciation. The Acheulean appearance of some of the Baker's Hole flints may possibly be due to the makers continuing to work for a time in this tradition, until, with the onset of a harsher climate, the industry fell back into a primary Levallois stage, but on the whole it seems more likely that this Coombe Rock deposit was a result of the Third, Penultimate, Glaciation.

At Frindsbury, a workshop-site found in 1924 on a chalk spur just beyond the 100-foot terrace of the Medway had some features in common with Northfleet. The tools are much alike, but the Frindsbury cores are badly struck and not faceted. Piles of raw flint were set out in order on the workshop floor; near one was a hammer-stone of tough quartzite, a rock foreign to the immediate area unless it had been picked up in a Thames-side gravel, while close to another were two finished hand-axes. A great many failures attended the workers' efforts, hundreds of badly struck flakes suggesting their inability to produce satisfactory tools from the cores. Another site at Bapchild near Sittingbourne in Kent observed in the late 1920s gives rise to certain problems. The convex cores with faceted butts, flake-tools and struck flakes came from a deposit of Coombe Rock but they were incorporated in the chalky sludge and had travelled with it, as abrasions on some of the specimens clearly testify. Some of the flints, however, are sharp and clean as though they had travelled but a short distance, and they are abundant in number and variety. A finely worked and unrolled anvil block of grey flint made by trimming a rough nodule is evidence that some working at least took place near by. The industry chiefly represented appears to be Mousterian, although Levalloisean flakes can be identified.

Of interest also is a workshop-floor or occupation level examined in 1934 by Mr J. Bernard Calkin on the surface of the 135-foot raised beach in Slindon Park, West Sussex. The surface of the beach, left high and dry when the sea retreated, was every-where covered by Coombe Rock: the 27 hand-axes, about 280 flakes or flake-tools and nearly 20 cores recovered belong to a late Acheulean industry, and as the material was nearly all unrolled and unbattered and there were traces of two possible fireplaces it appears that this community of hunters and fishermen lived on the beach strand just above the level of high tide. Elsewhere in West Sussex Mr Calkin was also able to examine the raised beach which at present lies at 70–90 feet O.D., and among the shingle he found thick flakes and cores of an early Clactonian industry—the most primitive flint industry recognized in Europe

Fig. 4

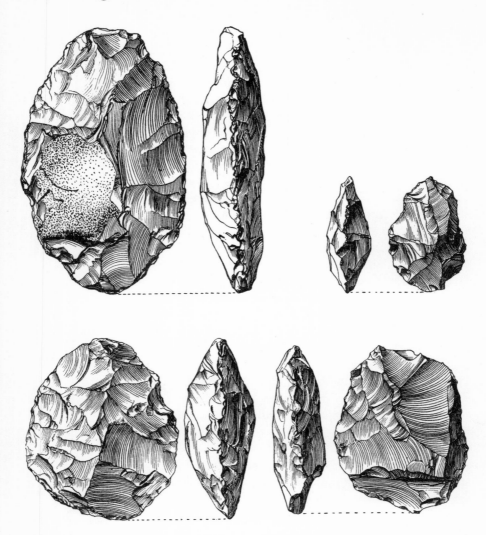

Fig. 4   Slindon, Sussex. Late Acheulean hand-axes, surface of 135 ft raised beach. Length of largest 4.9 ins

—all heavily water-rolled and some deeply scratched by ice. The inference must be that these tools were made before the glacial conditions which in turn existed before the formation of the raised beaches.

The grounds of Cuxton Rectory which lie on the 50-foot second-terrace gravel of the River Medway have long been known as a source of Palaeolithic implements. In 1962-3 the site was excavated and recorded with great precision by Mr P. J. Tester who recovered no less than 657 artifacts within an area of some 86 square feet. These included about 200 hand-axes (but only 360 waste flakes), together with cleavers, flake-tools and cores, many of which are clean and unrolled and must have been made quite close to the place of their discovery. Of particular interest are a few flake-scrapers which could have been used to shape wooden spears of the kind known from the unique example found at Clacton, and a hand-axe skilfully made from a nodule with a natural perforation, the purpose of which is obscure. No definite floors or horizons could be observed in the gravel or loam, and there was an absence of bones, shells and pollen which would throw light on contemporary life and climate. The typology of the implements, however, clearly points to a mid-Acheulean industry which on sound evidence from the Thames can be placed in the Hoxnian (Great) Interglacial, though there are difficulties in relating the Cuxton gravels precisely to the Thames valley geological sequence. It is thought that a near-by camp-site, which was in use on a seasonal basis over a long period, was from time to time flooded by the waters of a local stream: the small proportion of waste flakes to finished tools does not suggest a workshop of any size. In view of its obvious importance Mr Tester wisely left part of the site for future examination in the light of new techniques and research which will assuredly be available, and meanwhile it has been scheduled for protection by the Ministry of Public Building and Works. The flints, which are the only examples from a properly controlled excavation of a Palaeolithic

Fig. 5

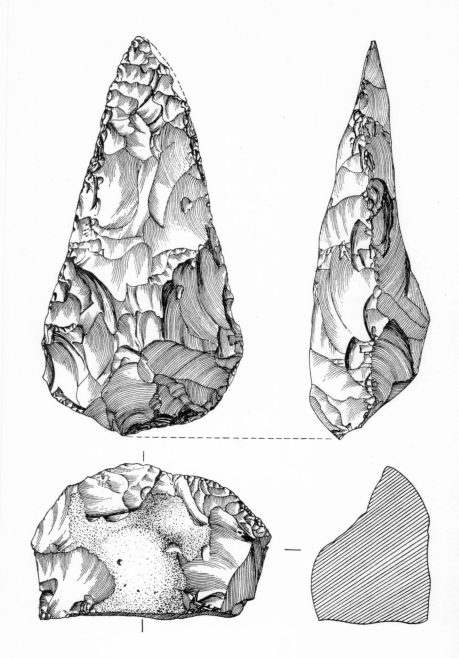

*Fig. 5   Acheulean site, Cuxton, Kent.
Left, hand-axe, length 8.5 ins, and chopper
of tea-cosy form, length 3.25 ins; right,
cleaver with tranchet edge, length 5.25 ins*

site in the Medway Valley, have been placed in the British Museum.

We are also indebted to Mr Tester for recent precise studies of the gravels of the Dartford Heath terrace and its contained flint industries. The geological age of the gravels is still a matter of opinion, but part at least must belong to the period of the Boyn Hill terrace, as is shown by Acheulean hand-axes of the same type as those abundantly represented in the Middle Gravel at Swanscombe. There can surely be little doubt that implements re-covered from the surface of the gravel and below the loam in the Bowman's Lodge pit were made during an interval towards the end of the Hoxnian Interglacial, but of greater interest is the association of typical mid-Acheulean hand-axes and cleavers with flake-tools exhibiting some Clactonian and Levalloisean techniques, and the presence of fitting flakes. All the tools were presumably made by men of the same cultural group, but there is at present no means of deciding whether the earlier techniques were used only in limited places and perhaps only from time to time. Something like Clactonian flaking, for example, can be seen on the much later Thames picks and even on Neolithic axes. Such important questions as these may well be answered in due course by the penetrating large-scale objective research into the Lower and Middle Palaeolithic hand-axe groups now being undertaken by Dr D. A. Roe. The mass of material available in south-east England alone is formidable, but his application of metrical and statistical analyses to the size, refinement and shape of implements will add much to our knowledge of typology and sequence.

The number of flint tools from recognized workshop-sites, large as it is in total, is altogether exceeded by the far greater number for which no such association can be claimed. Over a vast period of time, with great changes in the relative levels of sea and land and a wide variation in climate and living conditions, these almost indestructible relics became incorporated in the geological deposits accumulated by the natural drainage system at the various stages of its evolution, the constant main feature of which was the Thames and its many tributary streams. Such fluviatile deposits of gravels, sands and brick-earths and the underlying chalk rock have long had a commercial value in south-east England: paradoxically our knowledge of palaeolithic man was a direct result of the suburban development of London and the coming of the railways. By the middle of the nineteenth century Thames-side gravel was in demand for railway track ballast, while by the turn of the century the market among builders and contractors for lime and Portland cement—for the manufacture of which a large overburden of sand and gravel had to be removed from the surface of the prime material, chalk—as well as for sand, hoggin and bricks had increased on an un-precedented scale. To meet the demand for raw material, many pits and quarries were then and subsequently opened along the south bank of the Thames, in the valleys of the Medway, Kentish Stour and Darent, farther westward in the Farnham gravels of the Wey, and in the Arun gravels in Sussex. At the same time there was a growing and sustained interest in the story of primitive man, in the collection of the flint implements which had long since been recognized as his handiwork, and of the fossil bones of extinct animals. The collection of flints and bones was almost wholly unscientific: few records other than those of general locality were kept, and the longer the collector's pocket the better was his standing with the pit-workers who found the relics. It was not at all unknown for good forgeries and genuine hand-axes from other localities to be given the provenance of favourite pits.

It has been said that more than 60,000 flint implements were obtained from workmen in the Swanscombe gravel pits. One well-known collector of bones and flints, H. G. Stopes, went so far as to build himself a house near by the better to prosecute his researches: his collection, now in the National Museum of Wales at Cardiff includes more than 1000 hand-axes alone from North Kent. The early collectors obtained their implements from pit-workmen who dug by hand; in later years with the introduction of mechanical digging, finds were far less numerous and this point should be borne in mind in any statistical survey. It is of interest to recall that a flint axe found with mammoth bones in the gravels of the Wey as long ago as 1842 was then recognized as of human manufacture, a circumstance which deserves a minor place in the story of British archaeology.

By the opening of the twentieth century antiquarian studies had attained a more scientific approach, and in 1912 the British Museum in association with the Geological Survey made what has since become recognized as a classic investigation into the succession of human industries represented in the stratified deposits of the 100-foot terrace of the Thames. The Swanscombe Research Committee, convened under the auspices of the Royal Anthropological Institute, whose 1938 Report is further noticed below and to which reference must be made by everyone seriously interested in paleolithic studies, considered in detail all the various

aspects of Pleistocene geology and archaeology and put chronology on a firm basis.

Briefly, the general section through undisturbed gravels of the
100-foot terrace was found to be as follows:—

Feet O.D. 115   Upper Gravel and Hill-wash. A solifluction
deposit with clay matrix, perhaps the main
Coombe Rock phase.

110   Upper Loam. Decalcified sandy loam with
unworn white patinated Middle Acheulean
hand-axes. Surface at 110 feet O.D. Hoxnian
Interglacial, probably a late phase.

107   Middle Gravels and Sands. Clean yellow
sand at the top with gravelly layer at base
containing derived Tertiary pebbles, chert
derived from the Lower Greensand and
quartzite pebbles from the Trias of the Midlands. Fossil mammals and shells. Mid-
Acheulean hand-axes and flakes. The Swanscombe skull was found in a cut channel at
the base. Hoxnian Interglacial.

88   Lower Loam, weathered land surface. No
implements.
Lower Gravel with stones as in the Middle
Gravel. Fossil mammals and early Clactonian flakes, choppers and cores. Hoxnian Interglacial. Deposited in a wide shallow
channel cut in the underlying solid rocks,
Eocene Thanet Sand,

75   and Chalk.

None of the Clactonian flakes was scratched by ice as at Slindon,
but their distinctive dark-brown glossy patina suggests that they
too may have been derived from the previous interglacial period.

At Fordwich and Sturry on the Stour gravel workings provided a rich harvest of implements to local collectors. Many of the Fordwich flints are pointed hand-axes of primitive type, large and heavy and coarsely flaked, and must be among the earliest from the south-east of Britain. So far as it is now possible to tell they came from the base of a deep section of gravel. One collector alone had upwards of a hundred hand-axes and side-scrapers of Acheulean form from Sturry, but all were purchased from work-men. The four gravel terraces of the Wey at Farnham have also enriched the cabinets of many a collector, but there appears to be little in the way of strict archaeological evidence and some of the collections cannot now be traced.

Several sets of human bones found in the Thames gravels of north-west Kent have been regarded on various grounds as the remains of Palaeolithic hunters and food-gatherers. It is well to say at once that a skull discovered in 1902 in a gravel-pit at Dart-ford, in which many palaeoliths had come to light, another, it was said, from above the level of Coombe Rock in chalky gravel and close to the well-known Levalloisean workshop site in Baker's Hole, Northfleet, and yet others obtained by collectors from pits in the Swanscombe district, are not supported by satisfactory evidence of this very high antiquity. A similar caveat must be entered against a skull from the Medway gravels at Aylesford, and fragments of another from the Ouse gravels at Barcombe Mills, Sussex.

'Galley Hill Man', who quite wrongly became known as a new subspecies *Homo sapiens londiniensis*, has managed to achieve a degree of fame. The bones of an almost complete skeleton were found in 1888 by a gravel-digger 8 feet below the surface (it was said) in a pit dug in the 100-foot terrace of the Thames just west of Galley Hill, Swanscombe, from which Palaeolithic hand-axes had been obtained, and passed into the hands of an amateur col-lector at one of his usual fortnightly visits to the pit in search of flint implements. No account of the find was published until

7 years later. It was maintained by some authorities that the skull showed marked primitive features, though this was denied by others, and down the years there was lack of confirmatory evidence that the deposit in which the bones were found was in fact undisturbed. Boyd Dawkins, Duckworth, John Evans, Keith and Sollas all realized that such evidence as there was tended to point to the probability of a later intrusive burial, but in some quarters this modern type of skeleton was regarded as an indigenous fossil of the 100-foot terrace of the Thames, of Lower Palaeolithic age, and so antedating Neanderthal Man. The problem was indeed difficult. But by 1949 considerable attention had already been focussed on 'Swanscombe Man', a true fossil from this terrace, and more particularly Dr K. P. Oakley and Professor Ashley Montagu had been able to make a detailed geological and anthropological reconsideration of the Galley Hill skeleton. A re-examination showed that the bones do not present any primitive features whatever. While this is also largely true of the skull of 'Swanscombe Man', a study of the geological evidence at Galley Hill—unlike Swanscombe the deposit was almost completely decalcified by percolating water—strongly suggested that the bones there recovered were in all probability from a comparatively recent burial and this strong probability was confirmed by a controlled and comparative fluorine test which showed that the bones were of post-Pleistocene age. The relative dating results of the fluorine test were subsequently confirmed by a determination of the nitrogen-collagen content of the same bones. More importantly, in 1959, the direct age of the bones was determined by radiocarbon tests in the Research Laboratory of the British Museum as 3,310 BP± 150. This, it is thought, is the first instance in which supposedly fossil human bones have been directly dated by measurement of their radioactive carbon content. 'Galley Hill Man' is clearly not an indigenous relic, far less a new subspecies of *Homo sapiens*: he may represent an intrusive burial of the Early Bronze Age.

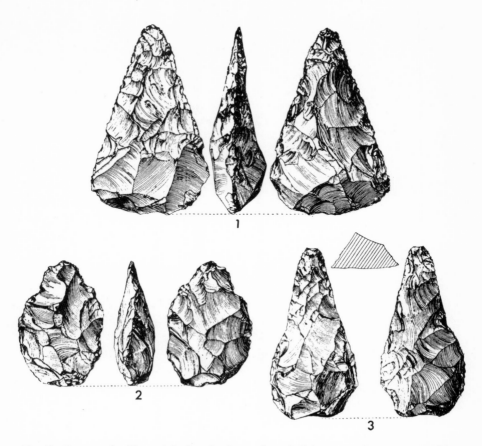

Fig. 6   Swanscombe, Kent. Acheulean hand-axes from skull layer. 1 and 2 near occipital bone. Length of 1 : 6.2 ins

If modern enquiry has put this man from Galley Hill in his proper place, it has also assured the status of 'Swanscombe Man'—the name is here used in a popular sense, and notwith-standing the fact that the remains were those of a young adult female—pieces of whose skull were likewise found in the im-plement-bearing gravels of the 100-foot terrace of the Thames and just over half a mile from Galley Hill. The story is one of the highlights of British archaeology.

For almost a century the Swanscombe gravel pits have been known as a source of supply to collectors of flint implements and bones of extinct animals, and it was as a result of the excavations already noted conducted by the British Museum and the Geological survey in the Barnfield Pit in 1912 that the succession of Palaeolithic industries in Britain was first adequately demonstrated. Much of the collecting since that date had continued to be quite unscientific, but very fortunately for British archaeology, Mr A. T. Marston, a London dental surgeon who was collecting in the pit in 1935 and who had always been alive to the possibility that sooner or later human remains might come to light, was able to treat his discovery with the care and importance it rightly deserved. He found, 24 feet deep at the base of the undisturbed Upper Middle Gravel of the 100-foot terrace of the Thames, the occiput of a human skull, and with continued and intensive effort he found the left parietal of the skull—and it articulated perfectly with the occiput—nine months later in the same seam of gravel. Full details of the discovery of the human bones, fossil animal bones and of unabraded flint hand-axes of Acheulean type found in the same deposit were recorded with meticulous detail. A Research Committee of the Royal Anthropological Institute was then convened, largely at Mr Marston's suggestion, to report on the discoveries from a specialist point of view, and although the Committee's own subsequent excavations did not reveal any further human remains its Report accepted the bones found by Mr Marston as those of the first completely authenticated indigenous human fossil of the gravels of the 100-foot terrace of the Thames, an individual of the Middle Acheulean hand-axe culture who lived in a late stage of the Great (Hoxnian) Interglacial. The unassailable evidence of geology, zoology, anthropology and archaeology all combined to assign to this fossil skull a very great antiquity. In view of its importance the site was designated as a National Nature Reserve by the Nature Conservancy, and as other human remains might

Plate 6

Fig. 6

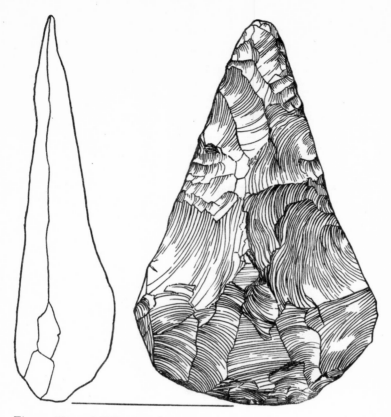

Fig. 7 Upper Middle Gravel, Swanscombe, Kent. Flint hand-axe in mint condition. Length 6.25 ins

well exist in the undisturbed area of the gravel still remaining, a programme of careful excavation was started in 1955 under the auspices of the Wenner-Gren Foundation for Anthropological Research and carried on for five years. By a fortunate chance Mr John Wymer and his associates discovered on the second day of their excavations the right parietal bone of the skull found by Mr Marston 25 years earlier. Meticulous excavation produced no less than 487 flint implements, nearly all in sharp and unrolled

Fig. 7

condition, 4831 primary flakes and 3316 finishing flakes and a rich and substantial mammalian fauna, all from a specific area. The implements included no fewer than 133 hand-axes, ranging in length from $6\frac{1}{4}$ inches to a diminutive $1\frac{3}{4}$ inches—was the latter a toy as Mr Wymer suggests?—which exhibit great variation in technique though all are certainly of an Acheulean industry. No doubt the source of the raw flint and the degree of the workers' skill determined the form of these cutting, stabbing, scraping, chopping and hammering tools and weapons. Some hand-axes may have been used in the production of bone or wood tools: there is no direct evidence but the large proportion of broken bone yielded by the excavation is suggestive. The number of flint flakes discovered is very large, so great indeed that Mr Wymer suggests that we must envisage a riverside beach strewn with waste flakes. The mammal remains gave reliable evidence for 26 species including straight-tusked elephant, rhinoceros, cave-bear, lion, horse, four species of deer, giant ox, wolf, and hare. The abundance of woodland species from the Lower Gravel is contrasted with the more open grassland fauna of the Middle Gravel. Bird remains were few, and there was but one fish represented, a pike from the Lower Gravel. No further human remains came to light and no occupation-site, but the excavators found traces of fires, whether natural or of human cause could not be determined.

Apart from the thickness of the parietals, the size, proportions and outline of the bones of the Swanscombe skull are in general much like those of a modern human, and no features of its endo-crinal cast serve to differentiate the brain from that of a modern man. It would seem therefore, on morphological evidence, that there was in Europe a type of Acheulean man whose bones are very similar to those of *Homo sapiens*, and that the species of *Homo sapiens* has a much greater antiquity than some anthro-pologists were hitherto prepared to allow. In any event, Swans-combe, the earliest fossil man in Britain, now appears to join the fossils from Steinheim (Germany), Fontechevade (France), and Ehringsdorf (Germany) as the oldest known examples of the species of modern man. Full information about the Swanscombe Skull is given in the 1964 survey of the Royal Anthropological Institute noted below and its bibliography of 113 items.

The Swanscombe skull together with a selection of the im-plements and the Galley Hill skeleton are in the collection of the British Museum (Natural History). A further selection of the Swanscombe implements may be seen in the British Museum.

This account must conclude with a note on Piltdown Man, that odd uneasy character, mixture of man and ape, who for many years dominated all discussions about prehistoric man in Britain. His remains, pieces of a very thick human skull, part of an ape-like jawbone with two teeth, together with bones of extinct animals, rough flint tools and a remarkable tool of bone had been found it was said in 1912 by Charles Dawson and Arthur Smith Woodward, in a deposit of gravel at Barkham Manor near Pilt-down Common, Fletching, Sussex, which it was claimed was laid down early in the Ice Age or even before. An ape-like tooth, worn down flat in a curious way, was produced a little later. This strange combination of man and ape, which was given the name of *Eoanthropus*, Dawn Man, was generally regarded as a new ancestor of man and it was thought that here at last was evidence of an ape-like man who lived early in the Ice Age, a missing link in human evolution, evidence which had been hoped for by many leading scientists, as well as, in a more limited way, by the Ightham Circle as proof of their case for eoliths. The discovery was given added value by the reported finding of further similar skull fragments and another tooth a few years later, not far from the site of the first discovery. Darwin's theoretical views on the ancestry of man thus received strong evidential support, and while there was always some difficulty in accepting the association of an ape-like jaw with the remainder of the skull, particularly in view of other discoveries of fossil man made abroad, *Eoanthropus* and his assemblage of animal bones and tools were held to represent the remains and associations of a primitive man who had de- veloped along a special isolated line of evolution.

There the matter remained with controversies from time to time until in 1949 fluorine-dating tests were applied to all the ver- tebrate specimens from the Piltdown gravel. It then became clear that the skull was not nearly as old as the extinct animal bones with which it had been associated, and Dr K. P. Oakley and Dr J. S. Weiner described it as an evolutionary absurdity and a 'grotesque and quite irrelevant dead end'. Further tests followed in which scientists using modern methods and equipment col- laborated. With detailed micro-chemical analyses, crystallo- graphic analysis, radiometric assay of uranium content, the use of X-ray spectrography and electron-microscopy, with practical experiments on analogous material, and with common sense, the problem of Piltdown Man was reconsidered.

These new studies confirmed beyond doubt that the Piltdown jaw-bone was that of a modern ape which had been most skilfully faked by staining and mechanical treatment so as to represent a fossil, and that the bones of the skull which was of a comparatively recent man had also been deceptively stained to give an appearance of vast age and put in the gravels there to be discovered. It was also proved beyond a doubt that none of the associated relics, the fossil animal bones—of the 18 specimens found six were definite and the remainder probable frauds, including an elephant tooth probably from Tunisia and a hippopotamus molar from Malta,— and the flint and bone tools, could have been genuinely found in the gravels with the skull. All these fraudulent relics had been placed there to suggest a primitive background, and to suggest that the skull belonged to an almost incredibly early period, the earliest phase of the Ice Age.

Piltdown, an amazing archaeological hoax for 40 years, can never be repeated. But the village inn, renamed 'The Piltdown Man' in honour of the discovery, bears the skull and two mammoths as its sign, a memorial to a lost cause, while Charles Dawson, the finder, was commemorated by a memorial stone not far away. His associate Lewis Abbott, remarkable amateur geo-logist, jeweller and curiosity-shop proprietor and the last of the original Ightham Circle, died in 1933 at the age of eighty. Some of us yet remember his volatile personality. The name of Venus Hargreaves, one of the Piltdown labourers, like that of the one-eyed Jumper Hutches who found four gold armlets under Beachy Head, has passed into the literature of Sussex worthies.

A little known but admirable day-to-day account of the Piltdown discoveries is included by Mr Ernest Raymond in *Please You Draw Near* (London, 1969), the last volume of his autobiography. Neither Dr Weiner nor the present writer feel able to name the probable perpetrator of the forgeries, but Mr Raymond leaves but little to his readers' imagination.

CHAPTER III

Hunters and Fishermen

THE SLOW RECESSION of the ice after the final glaciation made for a gradual improvement in climate and in time the south-east of England became part of an area clothed with thick Boreal forests of birch and pine which supported a varied and considerable fauna. Britain was still part of the continental land-mass. The Thames was a tributary of the Rhine which had its mouth by the present Dogger Bank; the land surface in the south was slowly sinking and incursions by the sea finally resulted in the separation of Britain from the continental mainland. Some-where about 5000 BC this gradual insulation was associated with a change in climatic conditions. The dry cold winters and warm summers of the Boreal gave place to the wet and mild weather of an Atlantic climate with a consequent change in flora and fauna. More specifically the main occupation at Oakhanger, a well-known Mesolithic site in eastern Hampshire not far distant from the Surrey border, occurred in an early part of the Atlantic phase, and carbonized hazel-nut shells gave a radiocarbon age determination of 6300 ± 120 years BP. The complete skeleton of an ox, found sealed under five feet of clay and with the remains of its last meal still present at Buckhurst Hill, Essex in 1967 may offer further possibilities of pollen analysis and radiocarbon dating.

The slow but over-all improvement in vegetation and thus in animal life was steadily followed northward and westward by hunting and fishing communities from the forests of northern Europe in their constant search for means of subsistence. Some of these Maglemosean peoples had crossed by way of the drowned pools and meres of the land bridge before the final and complete breaching of the Strait of Dover. Later, groups of Tardenoisean peoples from northern France and Flanders, ultimately perhaps from Northern Africa following the desiccation of the Sahara, crossed the narrow Channel and settled chiefly in the sandy regions of the south-east. These two groups of Mesolithic peoples, set against a background of the age-old Palaeolithic tradition, formed in the south-east a cultural influence which was to persist far into the Neolithic and even indeed into the Bronze Age of conventional archaeology.

An important site of early settlement was at Broxbourne, Herts in the fens of the Lea, a tributary of the Thames. Here were found Maglemosean flint tools sealed under a layer of peat shown by its pollen-content to have been laid down in Boreal conditions, perhaps about 6000 B C. Evidence from the later Atlantic period will be noted later in this chapter, but meanwhile it may be said briefly that the distribution of Mesolithic material emphasises the importance of the early Thames and its tributaries throughout the initial and subsequent phases of settlement. The use of dug-out canoes is clear from two wooden paddles found on an old coastal land-surface at Clacton, Essex, another (unpublished) with two flint tranchet axes at Swanscombe, Kent, and more importantly from an actual boat found in shelly marl below 5 feet of peat-covered clay at Sewardstone near Broxbourne. This boat, 13 feet long and with a 6-inch thwart and made from an oak trunk, is now in the Colchester and Essex Museum. Seven or more dug-out tree-trunk canoes of indeterminate date are known from the Arun valley and the sea-shore of Sussex, and there is recent news of another dredged from the river at Walton-on-Thames, Surrey. The Thames itself and the offshore southern waters of its estuary have yielded many hundreds of the long narrow tranchet-edged flint axes which would have been eminently suitable for this sort of boat-construction as well as for tree-felling. So familiar are these core axes, a feature of Maglemosean cultures, that they are widely known as 'Thames picks'.

Fig. 8

The natural environment of the sandy ridges of the Weald and some regions of the chalk country covered by later Tertiary sands were ideally suited to the nomadic food-gathering, hunting,

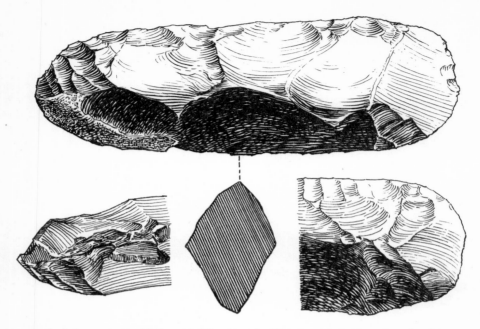

Fig. 8 'Thames Pick' of dark mottled flint from the Thames at Erith, Kent. Length 5.8 ins

trapping and fishing tribes of the Mesolithic. Well-drained hunting lands in a comfortable easy terrain with light forest cover provided natural animal food, skins and bones, edible fruits, berries and nuts, and the all-important timber for shelters, bark and resin products. The many springs and streams of the south-east gave ready supplies of water, contained fish and supported wild-fowl whose flesh and eggs probably gave variety to the food supply. Above all flint in nodules was readily obtainable from outcrops of chalk and as pebbles from more local spreads of gravel for the manufacture of the tools and weapons upon which the maintenance of human life depended. In their exploitation of these resources the Mesolithic peoples travelled over wide areas, to the thick forests on the Weald Clay, to the sands of the High Weald, to the chalklands, and it is possible to visualise a summer and winter seasonable occupation of their semi-permanent camping-places and settlements. The acid sandy soils of the main areas of settlement have destroyed everything but flint and stone. Not a single potsherd or piece of bone, human or animal, has yet been discovered, and only the waters and mud of the Thames have preserved a few fish-spears and mattock-heads of antler and bone. Here there is certainly no major site such as Star Carr in Yorkshire, but the evidence it has provided is in its way quite outstanding.

The very large number of small flint tools found in west Surrey has interested local antiquaries for almost a century. As long ago as 1880 Blackheath, Wonersh, which has since proved to be an extensive Mesolithic site, was a paradise for collectors—among whom was Pitt-Rivers—as were several other sites the finds from which went into private cabinets. Little serious attempt was made to understand the evidence until in 1933 Dr Wilfrid Hooper published a learned paper on the pygmy flint industries of Surrey, a paper preceded only a year earlier by Professor Grahame Clark's detailed study of the whole of the British material which four years later the same authority, in a classical work, put into its full setting in Northern Europe. The Mesolithic settlement pattern in west Surrey, St Leonard's Forest, Horsham, (a characteristic asymmetric hollow-based flint point, the Horsham point, was first recognized in this area by Clark), the Lower Greensand ridge in Sussex, and south-east England generally, was the subject of further studies over many years by W. F. Rankine who introduced into his own extensive fieldwork a system of transect excavation, notably at Kettlebury, Lion's Mouth, Frensham and Trottsford, whereby precise distributions were recorded and exact appreciations of industrial activity made. In more recent years Mr A. D. Lacaille has made valuable and detailed studies of the typology and distribution of Mesolithic cultures along the banks of the Middle and Lower Thames.

Much has been learned of the flint industries which formed the background to, and in the south-east yielded almost the only

53

traces of, daily life. Workmanship was generally of a high standard and technique equally highly developed with firm control of shape and purpose. There was some degree of selection in the raw material essential for such work, hence perhaps the popularity of Badshot compared with other sites where flint was equally accessible. Mesolithic techniques required large supplies of flint, and the manufacturing campsites are distinguished by the vast amount of waste material. At Oakhanger, one of the most prolific chipping floors in the whole of Britain, there were some 3,000 finished products among the 85,000 odd pieces of flint recovered. The industry, which may properly be called the Wealden industry to indicate its wide regional extension, is distinguished by its blade products which were obtained by both direct and indirect percussion from carefully prepared cores. Included in the range of blade and flake tools were microliths allied to the Tardenoisean of Continental Europe, scrapers, knives, saws, and gravers suitable for working in wood, bone and animal skin. Transverseflaked arrowheads are common in west Surrey but rare elsewhere: axes, scrapers, gravers and punches were fabricated from cores. Interesting products are the curious slender rodlike and spatulate microliths of uncertain use which occur occasionally, though 15 were recovered from the Farnham excavations, and the many cores which have been characteristically prepared for reuse. With resinproducing trees and an abundance of bark there would have been no difficulty in securing the small weapons and tools in wooden shafts and holders, themselves shaped with the flint tools available.

The variety of axes, choppers, javelinpoints, arrowbarbs and fishspear tips is sufficiently indicative of foodgathering communities almost entirely dependent for their livelihood on bush and treefelling and the subsequent use of their products. There is the interesting possibility that some well flaked discs were used as slingmissiles against birds: somewhat similar flints were so used in the Cambridgeshire fens in the nineteenth century according to George Glover, the notorious forger of flint implements.

The Greensand country at Addington, Kent, has long been known as a prolific source of Mesolithic implements and their debris. The well watered lightly wooded landscape within close reach of a tidal river and ready supplies of flint had obvious advantages for the food-gathering hunters and fishermen. The top of the Greensand, here white in colour, 5 feet below the surface has yielded burins, flakes and cores associated with a post-hole, and axes, gravers and microliths together with part of a sarsen stone mace-head were found under stratified peat containing lime pollen. The Mesolithic industry is probably a late one, not far removed in time from the building of the near-by megalithic tomb at Chestnuts. Another single post-hole sealed by the old ground surface came to light during the excavation of the megalith and both post-holes may have supported temporary wind-breaks or shelters of stakes and boughs as in the extensive settlement recently examined at Downton near Salisbury.

A Mesolithic working area was found on the old land surface under the Chestnuts megalith and its products occurred in the topsoil scraped up to form the mound. The main characteristics of the industry represented are the small number of microliths and their lack of variety, the absence of burins, the large number of core-scrapers, and the presence of saws, flake-axes and a large group of tools with retouching. The typology, and good stratigraphical evidence that only a relatively short time separated Mesolithic from Neolithic occupation of the site, indicates that the industry is a late one. It falls within the south-east English group of microlithic-macrolithic industries well represented at Downton, but has little in common with material recovered from the well-known sites at Farnham and Lower Halstow. Since Downton may have been almost contemporary with its local Neolithic community there is the possibility of a similar relationship at Chestnuts, and as Dr John Alexander points out

Fig. 9

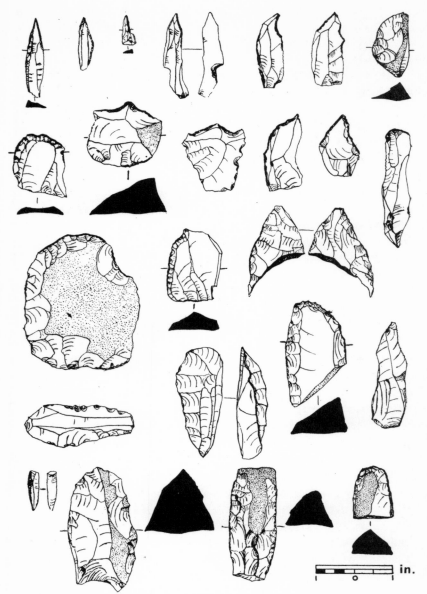

Fig. 9   The Mesolithic Industry, Addington, Kent

in his report on the excavation of the megalith the area may well have been visited by bands of Mesolithic hunters not very long before the burial-chamber was built. There were also suggestions of a working-site on the original surface under a bell-barrow excavated in 1960 at Deer Leap Wood, Wotton, on the Surrey Greensand. Indeed there is some support for the view that the barrow was built by people who lived in a Mesolithic continuum. Here also may be recalled the curious discovery many years ago of a Thames pick, tranchet-flakes and many flint daggers of conventional Bronze Age type at Pulborough on the Sussex Greensand.

For the rest, surface finds at Tovil, Hollingbourne, Allington, Ditton, East Malling, Larkfield, Seal and Ightham indicate the wide journeyings of Mesolithic peoples in their search for subsistence in the Medway region. The great number of tranchet-axes from the Thames and its estuary, and tranchets from the Sussex cliffs at Peacehaven, Seaford, and from the littoral at Portslade and Rustington, indicate water-borne lines of approach to the south-east, an approach which spread by way of the Stour, Medway, Darent, Mole and Wey gaps into the Weald, and far beyond into the south-west. It is not surprising that pebble tools of chert, quartzite and siltstone from the south-west and flint from East Anglia reached the south-east in return, though whether by way of trade or as a result of seasonal migration must be a matter of opinion. The Chesil Bank which was accessible to the Mesolithic nomads also provided a variety of raw material.

Shelter was of prime importance to the forestal hunting and fishing communities. At Balcombe in central Sussex, the sand below a rock-shelter in the Lower Tunbridge Wells Sand of the Wealden Series contained scrapers, saws, microliths—one a hollow-based point—a graver and working debris, all of the Wealden industry. Unfortunately the flints were not recovered by systematic excavation, but the association with charcoal suggests that this natural shelter may have been used in Mesolithic

Plate 7

Fig. 10

times. The sandy platform of the High Rocks escarpment of Tunbridge Wells sand in the same county gave the advantages of good drainage, a water supply and, more importantly, natural overhanging shelters of rock. It was used spasmodically by Meso-lithic hunters on a seasonal basis and later by casual Neolithic and Iron Age inhabitants, the latter probably associated with the hill-fort on the crest above. Excavations by Mr J. H. Money in 1954–6 yielded a variety of Wealden microliths typical of a hunter's bivouac. Charcoal from one site gave a radiocarbon date of 3780 ± 150 B P, but such a date it seems more properly refers to the settlement here of Neolithic hunters who were ap-parently using Ebbsfleet type pottery. Another radiocarbon date from a site is recorded as 3700 ± 150 B P, and pollen analysis does not contradict these findings. The zones from which the samples were taken contained 6 hearths, most of the flints of Mesolithic type and the main concentration of Ebbsfleet pottery. Three pit-dwellings excavated in 1933 at Selmeston, Sussex, on the Lower Greensand ridge yielded charcoal including oak of the late Boreal, flint pot-boilers and a large assemblage of late Mesolithic flint tools. It was thought from the typology of the flints that Selmeston was perhaps slightly earlier in date than the Wealden industry centred on the Horsham region, or that the differences between them could be attributed to regional variation of culture. The best preserved of these steep-sided pits in what was evidently a group settlement was oval in plan, about 15 feet by 8 feet and about 4 feet in depth. One pit, by then silted and out of use, gave very temporary shelter and a fireplace to later people using Peterborough-style pottery. A pit, perhaps a dwelling-pit, con-taining many Mesolithic implements was found at Hassocks in the same county.

A pit-dwelling at Abinger Common, Surrey, excavated by Dr L. S. B. Leakey in 1950 has happily been preserved by treat-ment with a silicon compound and given the protection of a wooden hut which also serves as a museum for its relics. Access

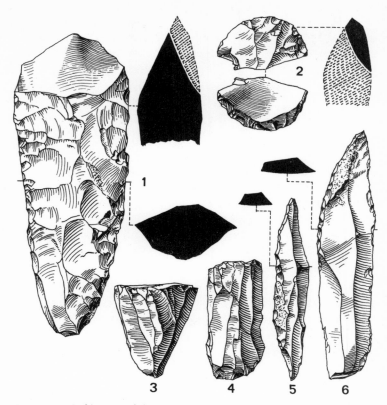

Fig. 10 Wealden Mesolithic Industries. 1, tranchet axe; 2, tranchet flake; 4, core; 5, steeply-flaked point, all from Selmeston. 3, core from Halland and 6, steeply-flaked point from Horsted Keynes. Length of 1 : 5.5 ins

to this interesting and important site is courteously given by the owner of Abinger Manor. The pit is again shallow, little more than 3 feet in depth in the natural Greensand, and its long and narrow outline measures about 14 feet by 10 feet. A sloping ledge along one side above its deepest point may have served as a sleeping-place, and a concentration of burnt stones and charcoal at one end may be the site of a cooking-hearth although two post-holes at the edge of the pit suggest stone-packed poles carrying a framework to support a roof of saplings thatched with grass or bracken or covered with animal skins. Some 1060 Mesolithic flints were found in the pit filling but the structure itself was surely too small for living and working quarters and is best regarded as a sleeping-place and shelter against bad weather. There is a spring close by, and the countryside would have had much attraction for hunters and food-gatherers.

Dug-outs or shelters below ground level were also found on a gravel spread close to the Lower Greensand at Farnham, Surrey, in an exceptionally accessible region with a good water supply which attracted prehistoric and Roman settlement and even now is a favourite stopping place for tramps. Four irregular shallow pits, systematically excavated by Professor Grahame Clark and W. F. Rankine in 1937–8, yielded a vast amount of archaeological material, one pit alone containing something like 15,000 worked flints. One solitary hole at the entrance to a pit probably held a post to support a roof of branches or turves, but there were no other structural features. Among some 1100 finished implements there were 690 microliths, 446 microburins, 26 gravers, 15 transverse-flaked axes, and siltstone pebble tools of south-western origin. Lumps of red and yellow ochre, extensive deposits of charcoal and the presence of carbonized hazel-nut shells add to the interest of this remarkable concentration of an industry set in the western Weald. Hazel-nuts here and at Selmeston suggest that the shelters were occupied in late autumn, and presumably they were winter quarters as against the temporary tents and other flimsy ground-level structures used in the summer hunting and fishing grounds.

The site of a temporary hunting camp on the Greensand at Iping Common, Sussex, totally excavated by the West Sussex Excavation Group in 1960–1 furnished a flint industry fully in the Maglemosean tradition. No less than 56 lb. of flintwork were examined, and with two minor exceptions all the tools and weapons were in a perfectly fresh condition. Detailed pollen

Fig. 11

Fig. 12

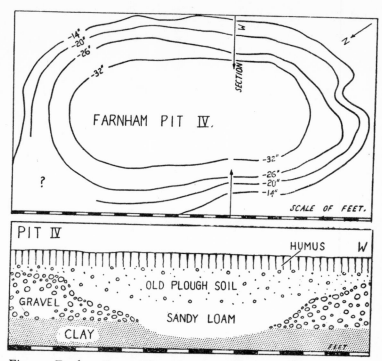

Fig. 11 *Farnham, Surrey. Plan and section of Mesolithic shelter site*

analyses showed the replacement of hazel woodland by heath, a change of vegetation brought about by the Mesolithic peoples during their occupation of the site. More information is likely to come from a site at Weston Wood, Albury, Surrey, which is now under excavation; here there are indications of a shelter near a clearly stratified hearth, and it is suggested that the flint industry falls late in the Wealden series, perhaps about 3500 BC, a date which may be confirmed by radiocarbon analysis of oak charcoal from the hearth.

The sour Greensand soil of the Weald preserved nothing but the stone industries of the Mesolithic peoples. It was otherwise in the lower valley of the Thames where from the river itself and its

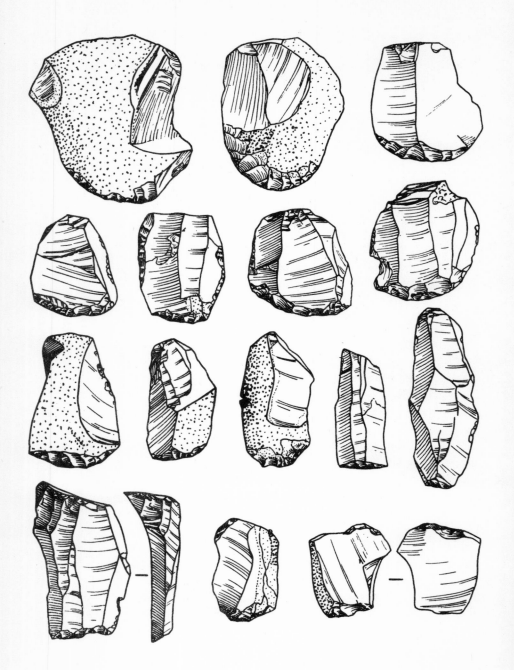

muddy foreshore an almost embarrassing amount of material has
been recovered. Apart from Broxbourne there are no stratified
sites and no scientific excavation has been carried out, and almost
all of the vast number of relics of this period—and others—are
collectors' pieces. Many objects from the Thames have passed into
the London, British and Reading Museums, while others have
have reached museums as distant as Edinburgh, Liverpool and
York. They have been recovered in dredging, diving and em-
banking operations; by unhandy watermen who put their craft
clumsily ashore; after the backwash of the Thames steamboats;
from excavated mud and gravel dumped far from its place of
origin; even from bottom-ice after a thaw. Scarcely a reach of the
river between Teddington and the sea has failed to yield its
antiquities, and it seems fitting that the Chairman of the Thames
Conservancy Board, which is responsible for the river from
Cricklade in Wiltshire to Teddington, should use as his gavel a
flint mace-head dredged from the river below Ravens Ait, Sur-
biton. A hammer-head with chevron decoration from Hammersmith, two barbed harpoons from Wandsworth and Battersea,
and two plain points from Battersea and Mortlake are bone
objects fully in the Maglemosean tradition, as are some half-a-
dozen antler mattock-heads from the middle reaches. These, the
numerous tranchet-axes and the fewer flake and blade tools are
fully described by Mr A. D. Lacaille in his welcome and up-to-
date survey of Mesolithic culture in the Lower Thames, referred
to earlier; he pays special attention to an evolutionary series of the
Thames pick tranchet-axes and allied forms, some of which were
modified to meet the particular needs of riverside inhabitants amid
growths of heavier trees. That much marshland now built over,
and higher land now represented by Ham Fields, Barnes and
Wimbledon Commons, supported vegetation suitable as cover
for game seems clear from the character of the mesolithic flints
found there. The appearance of the industries as a whole and
judged solely on their typology is a late one.

Plates 8, 9

Plate 10

*Fig. 12   Farnham, Surrey. Straight and convex scrapers from Shelter Site II.
Length of scraper at top left 2.3 ins*

Nearly fifty years ago as part of his research into the cultural age of the familiar Thames picks, Major J. P. T. Burchell excavated sites on the edge of Halstow Creek on the Lower Medway. Here, on redeposited London Clay, sealed by a layer of peat and covered by 6 feet of marsh deposits, he found tranchet-axes, microliths, awls, core-scrapers, a cupped sarsen pebble with hour-glass perforation, and the debris of flint-working. The sealing layer of peat contained pollen of alder, birch, elm, hazel, lime, oak and willow. There was no trace of pine, and as lime was already established, it seems that a Boreal climate had been replaced by damp and warm Atlantic conditions well after activity on the flaking-floor had ceased. Leaf-shaped arrowheads and polished flints were found very close to but outside the peat-bed in an area covered by 'landwash', while Iron Age and Roman pottery were also found near by. Further detailed examination of the stratigraphy of this important area would be worth while. The lagoon-like conditions under which the peat accumulated might well have preserved a settlement complementary in form if not in chronology to that of Star Carr.

No physical remains of the Mesolithic food-gatherers themselves have been found in south-east England. The discovery of pygmy flints and other relics associated with a cremated burial under a barrow at Seal near Sevenoaks, Kent, was recorded by Lewis Abbott who was concerned with Piltdown Man. The mound can still be seen, but the material and Abbott's remarks on it are indeed difficult to comprehend. Human bones found in 1912 at the base of the Medway alluvial loam at Halling, Kent, were formerly thought to be those of a Mesolithic man. Worked flints from above the loam were variously claimed as of Upper Palaeolithic, Mesolithic and Neolithic date. Recent radiocarbon dating of the femur at 4180 ± 190 BP indicates that it is most likely Neolithic.

CHAPTER IV

Farmers and Herdsmen

WHILE SOME OF the Mesolithic communities still pursued their nomadic life in the Greensand country and along the banks of the northern rivers, there arrived in the south-east a people who were to bring the beginning of settled life, a life based on mixed cereal and animal farming and embracing the art of pottery-making and a specialized practice of flint-working. They were part of a complex Western Neolithic group which included elements from the northern plain of Europe, from France and perhaps from Spain as well as from the south-west of England. The new arrivals with their characteristic tool the stone axe, particularly the polished flint axe, were attracted to lightly-wooded well drained areas of the chalk downs in the south and on the shore-line of East Kent. The North Downs and the South Downs towards the west, where tracts of heavy clay-with-flints supported a growth of thicker woodland, show few traces of their settlement. On the coast of East Kent casual discoveries of pottery and flint-work suggest that groups of these Neolithic people arrived directly by sea, and from this bridge-head they moved easily along the loam-terrains into the valley of the Kentish Stour. So far there is little evidence of major early settlement along the Medway and the banks of the Lower Thames; areas of gravel spreads and loams here may well have supported com-munities of farmers and herdsmen whose traces have been des-troyed by agricultural and urban development and by the com-mercial working of gravel and brick-earth. A dug-out canoe with a polished flint axe and a flint scraper on its floor found at Erith in the North Kent marshes may have belonged to such a com-munity. At Lower Halstow on the Medway, occupation of the Mesolithic site already noted may have continued into Neolithic times; however, the stratigraphical relationship between the two cultures is not entirely clear, and further investigation at Ebbs-fleet on the southern bank of the Thames is certainly desirable.

Once the downland trees and bushes had been felled by flint axes and wedges, firing and slashing of scrub, the breeding and grazing of cattle and sheep and the rooting of pigs resulted in a progressively further clearance. Small patches of land could be cultivated extensively though not continuously with the aid of flint hoes and soil-breakers, but no traces of the actual plots have yet been satisfactorily identified. The field-plots would be con-stantly moved as farmers sought new sources for fodder, and this movement was probably encouraged by a heavier rainfall and a water-level in the chalk appreciably higher than it is at the present day.

Discoveries in the south-west of England in recent years and their study by modern methods of research show that Neolithic settlement there was in progress somewhere between 4000 BC and 3700 BC, a date considerably in advance of that previously suggested. At Hembury in east Devon, an important settlement, a causewayed enclosure was occupied (on the basis of radiocarbon dating) between about 3320 and 3000 BC. Other settlements in the south-west, notably Carn Brea in Cornwall, and Maiden Castle, Dorset, have also produced acceptable evidence of such early date. Windmill Hill, long regarded as the type-site of primary Neolithic culture, must now, it appears, be regarded as a settlement of a south-western group of people with its immediate origins in western France, and a recent comprehensive study by Dr Isobel Smith has shown that the causewayed camp at Wind-mill Hill was not constructed until the Neolithic way of life was quite well advanced. The radiocarbon dating of the pre-enclosure Windmill Hill settlement has been determined at 2950 ± 150 BC. In Professor Grahame Clark's cogent words, the implications of recent developments for the ordering and nomenclature of the British Neolithic have hardly yet begun to be appreciated—'new knowledge can no longer be expressed by the old formulation'.

The period during which the south of Britain was occupied by Neolithic peoples has grown in length and importance. No longer is it to be seen wholly as a period of invasions but rather as a period when native evolution was taking place on a remark, able scale. That there was colonization from abroad is not to be doubted, but exotic novelties revealed by archaeology can be re, garded as an indication of increasing prosperity and standing at home as well as, and often rather than, signs of an incoming aristocracy.

The sites and monuments of what must here continue to be regarded as the primary Neolithic peoples in the south,east in, clude a distinctive form of earthwork known as causewayed enclosures, flint mines and factory sites, a few living,places often indicated by store,pits, and the earthen long,barrows of the dead. Megalithic tombs are discussed in the following chapter. Sussex archaeologists in particular have devoted much care and attention to recording and excavation and although there is as yet little in the way of an absolute chronology, much other information is available. And again for the sake of convenience the generally accepted terms of archaeological literature are used in the follow, ing pages, for it is too soon to envisage the amendments which are likely to follow a new appreciation of the British Neolithic.

CAUSEWAYED ENCLOSURES

These hill,top earthworks usually oval in plan consist of a con, centric series of ditches interrupted by causeways of solid chalk, the soil excavated from the ditches being piled up as a rampart on the inner side. Four examples are known on the South Downs. Whitehawk on Brighton race,course, excavated in 1929–35, has four concentric oval rings of interrupted ditches with known traces of a fifth and sixth, its outer area being about $11\frac{1}{2}$ acres with the inner ring enclosing rather less than 2 acres. The Trundle (that is the 'ring' or the 'hoop') at Goodwood, excavated in 1928–30, probably had three ditches, and the rampart behind the

Fig. 13

Plate 45

inner, which enclosed about 3 acres, still stands on the north to the imposing height of 7 feet. The maximum area of the enclosure was 18 acres. Outside the causewayed enclosure the hill-top is crowned with an Early Iron Age hill-fort, the Trundle proper. A similar hill-fort occupied the spur on which the causewayed enclosure at Hembury was located, and the Neolithic settlement came to light during the systematic excavation of the hill-fort. On Combe Hill, Jevington, the enclosure consists of two rings of interrupted ditches, the inner enclosing rather less than $1\frac{1}{2}$ acres, the outer now being incomplete. An interesting and unusual feature is the interruption of the inner ramparts which, apart from one sector, matches the interruption of the ditches. Excavation here in 1930 produced, again unusually, no primary Neolithic pottery at all but much belonging to a secondary Neolithic culture which will be discussed later in this chapter. The fourth enclosure is that on Barkhale Down, Bignor Hill; its single interrupted ditch and its rampart have been obliterated by ploughing, and this site too has produced secondary Neolithic pottery.

It seems that the occupants lived chiefly inside the inner enclosures, close to and in the ditches. There is no indication of structures, apart from the post-holes of a gateway on a causeway and those of two passageways through the ramparts at Whitehawk. Here the excavators found many of the post-holes of timber fences which stood on the top of the ramparts. The stratification of the silted ditches and their archaeological contents point to an intermittent seasonal occupation in contrast to the more permanent settlement at Hembury which may have lasted for some 300–500 years. At Whitehawk as well as in other causewayed enclosures the presence of grain-rubbers and querns indicates the practice of agriculture. The great quantity of domestic cattle bones, most of them of beasts not fully grown, and bones of pigs, sheep and goats point to the principal use of these earthwork enclosures as central stockfolds into which animals

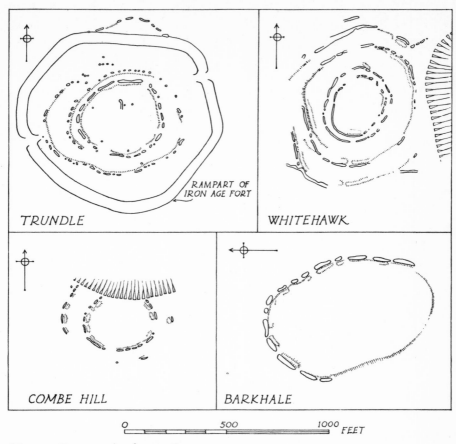

RAMPART OF
IRON AGE FORT

TRUNDLE

WHITEHAWK

COMBE HILL

BARKHALE

0   500   1000 FEET

Fig. 13   Causewayed enclosures, Sussex

were herded for breeding selection or slaughter at the end of the summer grazing season. Hazel nuts and crab-apples, the impression of grains of barley pressed into the clay of a Whitehawk pot while it was still soft, and perhaps the relative scarcity of fires all suggest the gathering of people in late summer or early autumn. Something in the nature of trading-centres or even fairs may be indicated.

69

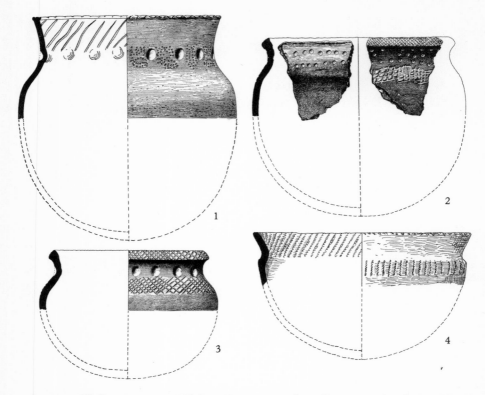

*Fig. 14   Ebbsfleet ware. 1–3, Ebbsfleet, Kent; 4, Combe Hill causewayed enclosure, Sussex.
Max. diam. of 1 : 5.5 ins*

The pottery recovered from the ditches belongs in the main to the round-based bowls of the Windmill Hill culture, and it has been suggested that some of the Whitehawk baglike bowls based presumably on hide and skin prototypes may owe something to Mesolithic vessels made of those materials. But with this A2 pottery were a few decorated sherds which Professor Piggott recognized as belonging to the second great series of British Neolithic pottery, the Peterborough family. Further, sherds of pots in the Ebbsfleet style, so known from its type-site on the Thames in North Kent and generally accepted as part of the secondary

Plate 18

Fig. 14

70

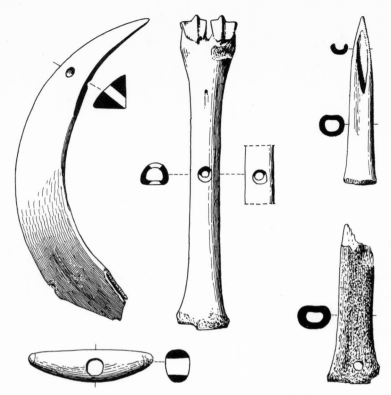

Fig. 15 The Trundle, Sussex. Bone points and tools. Length of bone comb 4.7 ins

Neolithic settlement, were intimately associated with the earliest occupation of the Whitehawk enclosures.

The pottery from the Trundle is exclusively of Neolithic A type, but even here there are suggestions of decoration more at home in an Ebbsfleet context. The emphasis at Combe Hill with its curious construction is absolute: among a thousand sherds of Ebbsfleet ware there is not a single piece of Neolithic A. There is similar ceramic evidence at Barkhale, as we have already noted. On these grounds alone a restatement of the chronology of the south-eastern causewayed enclosures is necessary.

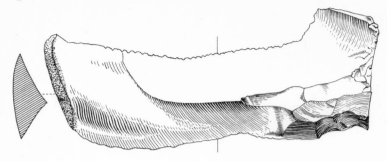

A new study of the flint and bone industries would support this view. Combe Hill yielded a leaf-shaped arrowhead, a scraper, many flakes and two sandstone grain-rubbers. Flint work at the Trundle was poor and scarce. There were leaf-shaped arrowheads, a roughly shaped axe, and saw-blades polished by contact with wood. At Whitehawk there were polished axes and rough axes; scrapers; lozenge, leaf-shaped and petit tranchet arrowheads; and more than 200 saw-blades. Here as at the Trundle were grain-rubbers and bone points for sewing skins or decorating pottery. At Whitehawk, too, the inhabitants used *Fig. 15* antler combs for removing hair from animal skins.

There are a few intimate sidelights on human life. Cannibalism and the eating of human brains at Whitehawk went side by side with the ritual, perhaps sacrificial, burial of a young woman and her child in a rough cist of chalk blocks accompanied by chalk pendant ornaments and two fossil sea-urchins as spells or periapts. In contrast, another slim long-headed girl and six other people had been flung into the ditch among domestic refuse. There were also burials apparently marked by wooden posts: the concept of the human soul upholding a post is not unknown in other primitive communities. A phallus of carved bone from the *Fig. 16* Trundle, if it is not to be regarded as a broken pendant, is evidence of a fertility cult, but whether perforated chalk blocks at

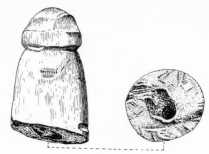

Fig. 16 The Trundle, Sus-sex. Flint saw left, and bone phallus. Length of saw 5.9 ins

Whitehawk, one weighing 32 lb., denote a system of weights must still be a matter of opinion.

The newly reported discovery of a causewayed enclosure at Lawford near the Essex Stour suggests that the distribution in the south-east may be wider than had been supposed, as does a now destroyed site at Chalk near Gravesend on the south bank of the Thames.

FLINT-MINES

In the Neolithic farming and stock-raising communities axes of flint or stone were the key features of existence and development. For forest clearance, the building of shelters and houses for the living and in some regions for the dead, the construction of primitive canoes and sledges alike, a constant supply of axe tools was an absolute necessity for the continuance of daily life. This must have been so from the time of the earliest settlements and subsequently over a very long period, even in competition with metal. It cannot have been long before the specialized flint-workers realized that flint newly obtained from the chalk was more suitable for their purpose than flint lying on the surface, and from open-cast mining in natural outcrops of chalk the development of shaft mining would have represented a natural progression.

The specialization in flint-working was not in itself static. There can be little doubt that in due course it derived fresh impetus and direction from contact with peoples who were familiar with the working of metals. It would seem that the products of the flint-mines did not reach Windmill Hill until a late stage in its history and Dr Isobel Smith has pointed out that there is no clear evidence of its contact with the primary occupation of that site. Further, two Sussex mines have produced evidence of an association with the makers of Beaker pottery, and one group may have been worked as late as the conventional Middle Bronze Age.

Plates 11, 12

Fig. 17

On the South Downs five flint-mining sites have been excavated at Cissbury, Harrow Hill, Blackpatch Hill, Church Hill at Findon, and Stoke Down, and there are two other sites, one on Windover Hill and the other at Lavant, which are probably mines. It will be noticed that the pattern of distribution follows that of the causewayed enclosures. Further to the north there was a surface flint-mine at East Horsley in Surrey, though its prehistoric date seems doubtful, and there are said to be filled-in shafts near Farnham in the same county. The many shafts in Kent generally known as dene-holes are not Neolithic mines as was once supposed; most are recent and comparatively recent marling pits, and the pick marks they exhibit were not made by antler but by metal tools.

Plate 14

Fig. 18

Plate 13

The Sussex mines, four of which have been excavated, and which are in groups of as many as one hundred, sometimes reach a depth of 50 feet and radial galleries at the bottom of the shafts dug to follow particular seams of flint traverse quite long distances and frequently communicate with one another. The shafts appear to have been filled in one by one soon after they were abandoned for more prolific neighbouring areas, and their appearance today is generally a series of hummocks and shallow depressions. Tools used by the miners included lever-picks, hammers and wedges of deer-antler and shovels made from the shoulder-blades of ox, deer and pig which were sometimes

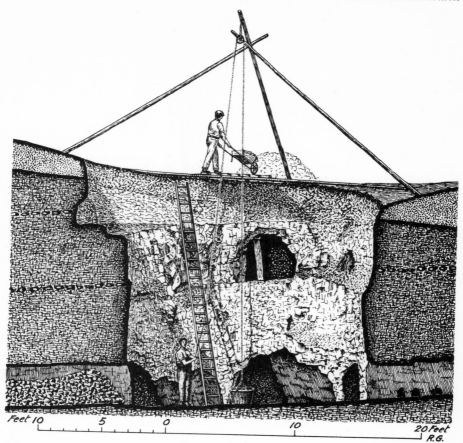

Fig. 17 Harrow Hill, Sussex. Section of flint-mine shaft and galleries

furnished with antler handles. Factories and flaking-floors were
close to the mouth of the mine, and the vast quantity of waste
flakes is an indication of the magnitude of their output. The
characteristic product is the long narrow and thin-butted axe
which occurs in every stage of manufacture though finished tools

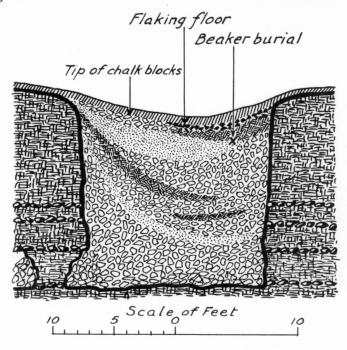

Fig. 18   Church Hill, Findon, Sussex. Section of flint-mine shaft

Fig. 19

are naturally less in evidence. Choppers and wedges were also made in quantity. No polishing was undertaken at the factories, but fine work with pressure-flakers of antler and presumably of wood reached a high standard. Interesting details are scratched tally-marks on the walls of the galleries at Harrow Hill, antler combs, perhaps for raking the rough-outs into heaps, and the soot-stains left by the miners' chalk cup-lamps.

The infilling of the shafts contains little domestic rubbish beyond the bones of animals used for food. Here and there we find some archaeological evidence of date. A friction-polished

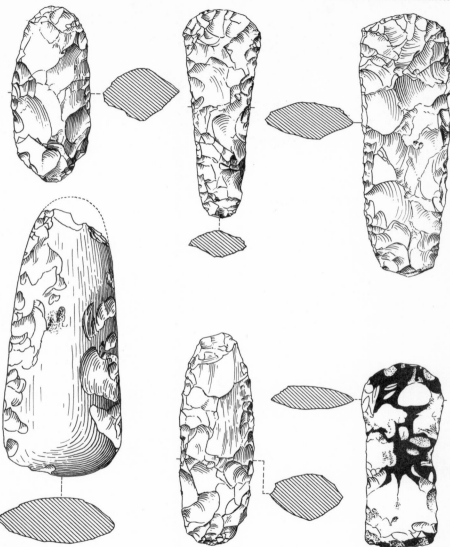

Fig. 19   Cissbury, Sussex. Flint-mine axes. Length of axe at top right 6.1 ins

Fig. 20 Cissbury, Sussex. Restored bowl from flint-mine shaft. Max. diam. 5 ins

Fig. 20

Fig. 21

sickle and part of a Neolithic A bowl were found at Cissbury, and an unusual tall oval beaker inverted over cremated bones and associated with two long axes was sealed in the upper filling of a shaft at Church Hill, Findon. Other discoveries of Neolithic and Bronze Age pottery appear to have been made at Findon and there is mention of a decorated wooden bowl and patterns left by the decayed rungs of a timber ladder. Most interesting of all is a series of eight burials in or near the mines at Blackpatch. A barrow containing the cremated remains of a child accompanied by a collared urn, two small flint axes and an oval flint knife perhaps deliberately broken had been built over the mouth of a shaft soon after it had been filled. Three other barrows produced among them cremation and inhumation burials, a collared urn, a leaf-shaped arrowhead, hand-axes and choppers, and all were clearly contemporary with various phases of the mining and factory industry. In wide terms this industry lasted from the early Neolithic until the middle of the conventional Bronze Age, and perhaps continuously. Its products were traded widely over the south-east, but in a lesser degree to the west country which had its own axe-factories. Three fine axes in mint condition lost perhaps on their way to their destination were found in 1937 at Peaslake, Shere, Surrey, and a hoard of eight came to light many years ago near Hurstpierpoint in Sussex.

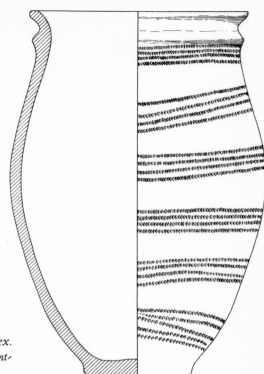

Fig. 21   Church Hill, Findon, Sussex. Beaker inverted over cremation in flint-mine shaft. Height 9.5 ins

The outward supply of flint axes was paralleled by an inward trade of axes, axe-hammers and maces made of fine-grained igneous rocks. They are in small numbers, just over thirty in south-east England, and of the twenty-two from Sussex no less than nineteen found their way into one private collection. Such axes and maces were surely objects of value and prestige, and it may not be accidental that many are of greenstone, the colour of weathered bronze and examples of 'that blessed viridity whereby all things germinate'. Petrological examination has shown that

several of the greenstone axes came from a restricted area in the Mounts Bay region of Cornwall, perhaps from a factory site now submerged. An axe of porcellanite found at Sittingbourne in Kent came from a factory at Tievebulliagh in Antrim. An axe of tuff from the Pike O'Stickle factory at Great Langdale in West morland was found at Frensham, Surrey, and another at Egham in the same county. An axe hammer of quartzite from the Whin Sill area of Northumberland came to light in Guildford, Surrey. These examples, casually found, and the one greenstone axe from Grovehurst, Kent, to be noted later, are all too few to fit securely into the chronology suggested by Professor Stuart Piggot in the final report of the Sub Committee of the South Western group of Museums on the petrological identification of stone axes. The range of cultural contacts is shown further by
Plate 15 magnificent jadeite axes from Canterbury, Mortlake on the Thames, Chilham and Deal—the last two in private collections now unfortunately dispersed—whether the rock source be Brittany, Piedmont in Italy or the Swiss side of the Alps.

LONG BARROWS

The usually casual disposal of the dead in the causewayed enclosure at Whitehawk is in strong contrast to the care and time which must have been expended on the ceremony and construction of the communal earthen non megalithic long barrows of which there are thirteen existing and one known destroyed example in south east England. Situated in conspicuous positions on the chalk downs, they form one of the outstanding features of the landscape. Of the twelve in Sussex nine are to be seen on the eastern downs between Whitehawk and Combe Hill, while the other three are situated near the causewayed enclosure at the Trundle. All are within easy reach of river gaps and flint mines. Some of the Sussex barrows have been dug into by treasure seekers, but none has been scientifically excavated. The largest is
Plate 19 the fine example Baverse's Thumb or Solomon's Thumb, near

Up Marden, first recognized by Mr L. V. Grinsell, which is just over 200 feet in length, some 60 feet in width and stands 7 feet high at its higher end. Many are much smaller. In general the mounds belong to one of the well-known varieties found in southern Britain, those with flanking ditches which are sometimes continuous, and as is common elsewhere, one end usually higher than the other. In no case is there present knowledge of associated or underlying timber structures. A pair of small long barrows on Stoughton Down in West Sussex have between them a possible round barrow.

The site of an isolated long barrow near Badshot Farm at the western end of the Hog's Back ridge in Surrey was excavated in 1936. The mound had been levelled by ploughing, but parts of the ditches were identified. Between the ditches, on an entrance causeway, was the hole of a seemingly ritual post. Sherds of Neolithic A and Neolithic B pottery came from the ditch, and there were two leaf-shaped arrowheads, part of a polished flint axe and ox bones split for their marrow. The interest of the site lies chiefly in its isolation from other long barrows and chambered tombs. Though Baverse's Thumb lies twenty-one miles to the south-west and there are two Wessex long barrows within almost the same distance, the next nearest, the Medway group, are 55 miles away. The North Downs Trackway may have served as a geographical link.

The remaining earthen long barrow, Julliberrie's Grave on the chalk downs overlooking the Great Stour at Chilham in Kent, owes its name and its folk-history to Camden. Several treasure-seeking antiquaries had dug into it before a more careful excavation in 1936–38 revealed part of its archaeological story. The north end has disappeared into a small chalk-pit, but the barrow may have stood on the edge of the chalk cliff bounding the River Stour; it is here 48 feet wide, tapering by 6 feet to its southern end with a present length of 144 feet and a maximum height of 7 feet. No ditch is now visible but it was traced around

Plates 20, 21

Fig. 22

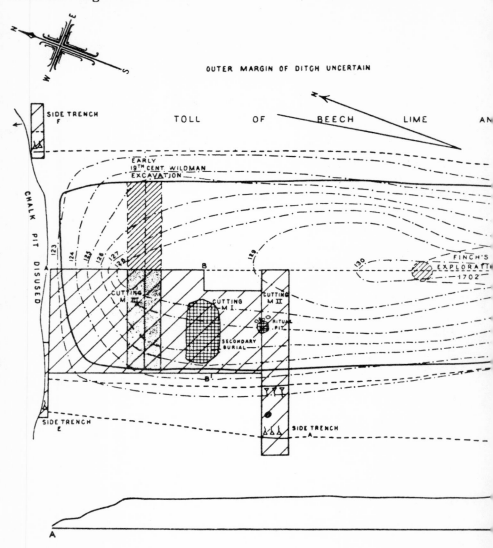

OUTER MARGIN OF DITCH UNCERTAIN

SIDE TRENCH F

TOLL OF BEECH LIME AN

CHALK PIT DISUSED

EARLY 19TH CENT. WILDMAN EXCAVATION

FINCH'S EXPLORAT 1702

123 124 125 126 127 128

129 130

CUTTING M III

CUTTING M I.

CUTTING M II

RITUAL PIT

SECONDARY BURIAL

SIDE TRENCH E

SIDE TRENCH A

Fig. 22   Julliberrie's Grave, Chilham, Kent. General plan

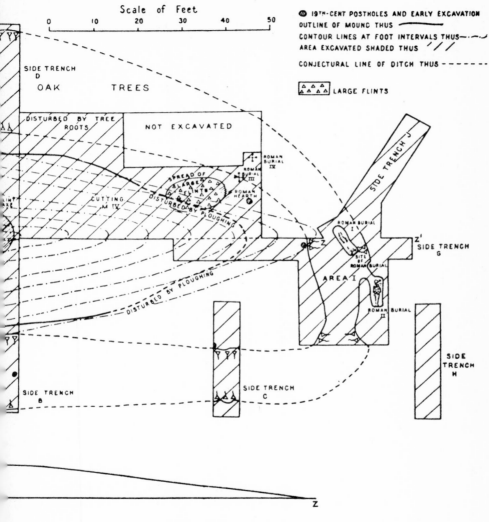

Scale of Feet

0   10   20   30   40   50

19ᵀᴴ-CENT POSTHOLES AND EARLY EXCAVATION
OUTLINE OF MOUND THUS
CONTOUR LINES AT FOOT INTERVALS THUS
AREA EXCAVATED SHADED THUS
CONJECTURAL LINE OF DITCH THUS - - - - - - -

LARGE FLINTS

SIDE TRENCH D

OAK   TREES

DISTURBED BY TREE ROOTS

NOT EXCAVATED

CUTTING M IV

SPREAD OF LARGE FLINTS

DISTURBED BY PLOUGHING

ROMAN BURIAL IV
ROMAN BURIAL III
ROMAN HEARTH

SIDE TRENCH J

ROMAN BURIAL I

Z' SIDE TRENCH G

SITE OF ROMAN BURIAL

AREA I

DISTURBED BY PLOUGHING

ROMAN BURIAL II

SIDE TRENCH B

SIDE TRENCH C

SIDE TRENCH H

Z

PROFILE ON LINE A-Z
SCALE AS ABOVE

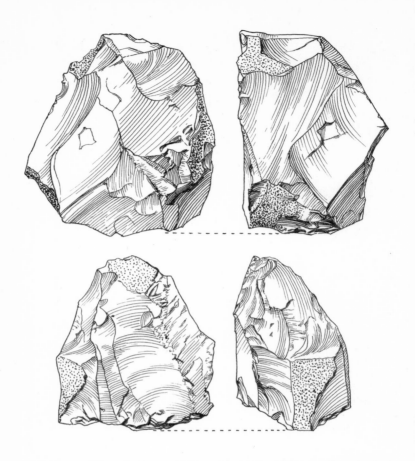

*Fig. 23 Julliberrie's Grave, Chilham, Kent. Above, flint cores from ritual pit;
below, from main silting of ditch. Length of larger 3.2 ins*

the barrow except at the destroyed north end. At one point in
the ditch, in its upper filling, four Roman burials had been
made at about AD 50, and marked by a small cairn of flints. At
the top of the filling under the present turf-line was a scatter of
eight late fourth-century Roman coins, part of a hoard in a pot
found in making post-holes for a fence early in the nineteenth-
century. Roman relics are associated with seven other earthen

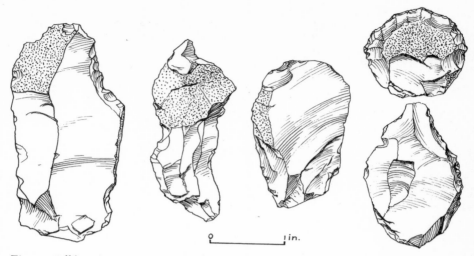

Fig. 24 Julliberrie's Grave, Chilham, Kent. Flakes and scrapers from ritual pit and main silting of ditch. Length of large flake 3.1 ins

long barrows in southern Britain as well as at Money Mound, a Beaker-period barrow at Lower Beeding, Sussex, and there is something to be said especially at Money Mound for a persistence of religious interest in the sites. At Chilham the mound which was made of surface soil and chalk from the ditch, had a core of turf and a pit in which no relics were found had been carefully sunk into the mound shortly after its completion. A ritual pit containing minor flint work and marked by large flint nodules was contemporary with the building of the mound. By far the most important discovery was made in the inner turf core: a fine though damaged polished flint axe with a thin butt of a type characteristic of the Nordic regions of Scandinavia, north Germany and Holland and there in use about 2000 BC. (A similar axe is known from Canterbury but it has no exact provenance.) It can scarcely be doubted that this damaged axe was deposited with ritual purpose. Its relative chronology may have to be amended—and there were no other objects of associated chrono-

Figs. 23, 24

Fig. 25

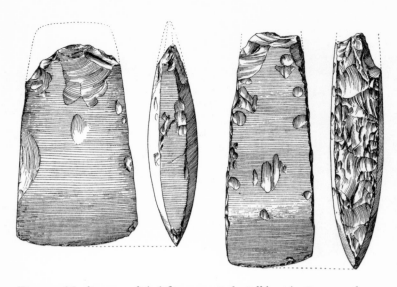

Fig. 25   Nordic type polished flint axes. Left, Julliberrie's Grave, turf core, length 5.4 ins; right, Canterbury, length 6.3 ins

logical significance apart from two small sherds possibly of Neo‐lithic A pottery in the primary silt of the ditch—but there can be little doubt that it entered the south‐east by way of the coast and the river‐system of the Stour as part of the elements in a settlement strongly marked in the region of Deal and Folkestone. A direct connection with the Sussex earthen barrows or with the well‐known earthen long barrows of Wessex seems unlikely: serious field‐work in the long‐neglected downland of East Kent may yet produce further evidence of long barrows. It is only necessary to add that no trace of stone or timber work was found in Julli‐berrie's Grave (though the northern end where the burials were presumably located was not available for examination) and that the builders could have had access to a local supply of sarsen stone had they been so minded.

This is not the place to discuss the origins and interrelationships of British long barrows. The megaliths of Kent will be described in the following chapter and here we must be content to commend Dr Glyn Daniel's observation that one of the fascinations of study, ing megalithic monuments and their non-megalithic prototypes and analogues is the varied interaction of both Northern and Southern traditions.

If it is asked in what sort of places the Neolithic agriculturists of south-east England lived, the answer which can be given at present is not very satisfactory.

The so-called hut-circles and pit-dwellings described by nineteenth-century antiquaries at Hayes, Ightham and Keston in Kent and at Shirley, Worm's Heath, Croham Hurst and else- where in Surrey, for example, yielded no evidence at all of their supposed age. Nine of the pits in the Ightham group in an area well known for its many surface discoveries of Neolithic flints were examined in 1933, when the excavators showed that the hollows were nothing more than sand-pits. A piece of what appears to have been Peterborough pottery came from a store-pit at Wisley, Surrey, and close to Redhill railway-station two circular patches from which cores, flakes, two leaf-shaped arrowheads, burnt flints and burnt bones were obtained in 1860 sound much more like the sites of barrows than of hut-circles as they were once thought to be. Nearly a thousand pieces of flint including cores, worked flakes and waste flakes were found in 1897 within a circular area on the Common at Millfield, Keston, but the illustrations of 9 blades suggest a Mesolithic context, as is indeed probable, and there is nothing whatever to support the contemporary postulation of a Neolithic village.

An oval store-pit or hut-floor on New Barn Down within a short distance of the Harrow Hill flint-mines produced little evidence of its structure when it was excavated in 1933 but it contained pieces of the familiar round-based bowls, a sandstone quern, an axe of the type and technique produced at the mines and a polished axe. Several more opened close to the Black Patch mines also contained axes, scrapers and flakes of flint-mine type, together with grain-rubbers of sandstone, animal bones and other refuse from a domestic hearth: little is known of the pottery said to have been recovered. In the Selsey peninsula, the in-filling of saucer-shaped depressions, the largest 10 feet in diameter and 2 feet deep, yielded part of a Peterborough-style bowl as well as pottery which could be attributed to the primary Neolithic settlement.

There are indications that a settlement existed in the valley of the Ebbsfleet, the stream which flows into the Thames at Northfleet, Kent. Excavations in the bed of the stream in 1938 produced at the base of the sealed alluvium many decorated, and a few undecorated, sherds of pottery which appear to be related to the Peterborough phase of Neolithic culture. Whether the culture was to be formally styled 'Mesolithic' or 'Neolithic', Professor Piggott said at the time, was a matter of pure nomen-clature rather than an important cultural distinction. With in-creased knowledge it can now be said that Ebbsfleet ware was found in the primary levels at Windmill Hill and at Whitehawk, both of which sites belong to the middle Neolithic of southern Britain. The excavations in 1938 were properly conducted, but Ebbsfleet has long been known to collectors and some of the many antiquities allegedly found there are clever modern forgeries.

A settlement of 'Secondary Neolithic' people at Grovehurst near Sittingbourne in Kent on a ridge of land rising some 50 feet above the surrounding marshland of the Swale has become well known from a most interesting series of antiquities found there between 1871 and 1890 in digging for brick-earth. The best preserved of the huts, of which a series was found, a bowl-shaped depression about 4 feet deep and 10 feet in diameter, was filled with layers of burnt and decayed vegetable material, and although no evidence of structure was recovered or perhaps at that time even looked for, we can agree with the excavator's

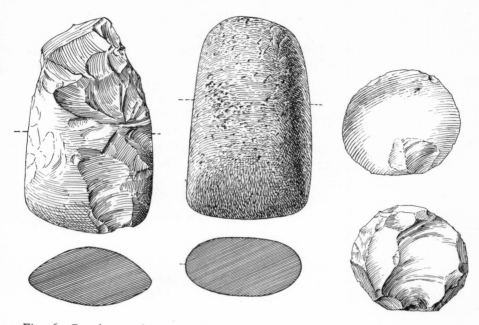

Fig. 26 Grovehurst settlement, Kent. Left, polished re-worked axe of non-local flint, length 4.7 ins ; centre, greenstone axe, length 4.4 ins ; right, flint scraper, max. diam. 3.5 ins

suggestion of wooden structures thatched with turf or reed. Remains of wattle-and-daub still preserved among the Grovehurst relics add an acceptable confirmation that these hollows are more likely to have been huts than abandoned and filled-up store-pits. Some evidence of the way of life is furnished by the bones and horns of cattle and by sandstone grain-rubbers, while the large number of flint tools and waste flakes and the occurrence of sandstone grinders and polishers and small spherical balls of much-battered flint indicate rather more than a domestic stone industry. All the relics from the site were recovered by sifting the bottom layer of the vegetable material on the hut-floors. Among the tools were seven pieces of fine polished axes of a grey non-local flint, several re-worked with coarse flaking, nearly all of pointed

Fig. 26

oval section, with thin butt and rounded cutting-edge. A carefully flaked curved sickle of grey flint, its inner edge polished by
friction with ripe corn stalks, and fragments of two others, a
remarkably fine almost transparent leaf-shaped arrowhead,
another of the same type, a tanged arrowhead, plano-convex
knives, and a boldly flaked flint-mine type of pick of local flint
retaining the natural crust at the butt and with peripheral, not
transverse, flaking on the cutting edge, together with a large
series of scrapers and blades both serrated and plain with and
without retouching, give an indication of the nature and range
of the other flint tools and weapons recovered. It is a strange and
in some ways inconsistent assemblage (notably the plano-convex
knives) in which products made with supreme skill and technique
are to be contrasted with those of inferior workmanship and in
which finely polished flint axes appear to be deliberately broken
and disfigured by rough flaking.

Fig. 27

Of particular interest is a short clumsy wedge-shaped axe of
unpolished greenstone, foreign to south-east England, which
has a thick rounded butt and a blunt almost straight-line cutting
edge. Another axe of exactly the same type and of almost the
same dimensions now in Maidstone Museum was found in the
same area. The cultural significance of axes of foreign stone has
been noted, but here attention should be drawn to the prevalence
at Grovehurst of non-local grey flint which can be matched in
Lincolnshire and in Belgium, and of which material there are
notable polished axes from Bexley, Harbledown, Margate and
Shorncliffe in Kent, each place having easy river or coastal access.

Fig. 28

One of the Bexley axes, found in a hoard of five which included
chisel-forms, is 11 inches in length and is clearly a ceremonial
object. The Shorncliffe axe is of nearly the same size.

Fig. 29

A few small pieces of pottery are among the material from the
Grovehurst huts which came eventually to the British Museum,
but in no case is there sufficient to attempt the reconstruction of a
vessel. This reddish-grey ware is tempered with grit and quite

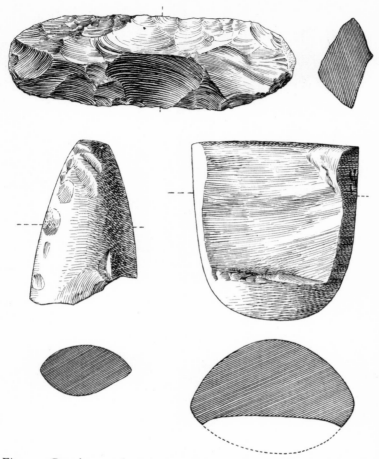

Fig. 27 Grovehurst settlement, Kent. Above, pick of black local flint, length 4.2 ins; below, polished and damaged axes of non-local flint, lengths 3.8 and 4.1 ins

well fired, the only decoration, a row of perforations below the rim, being on the fragment here illustrated. There is no evidence of the apparently flat-bottomed 'basins' mentioned in the first account of the discovery. The pottery has been variously claimed as belonging to both primary and secondary cultural groups.

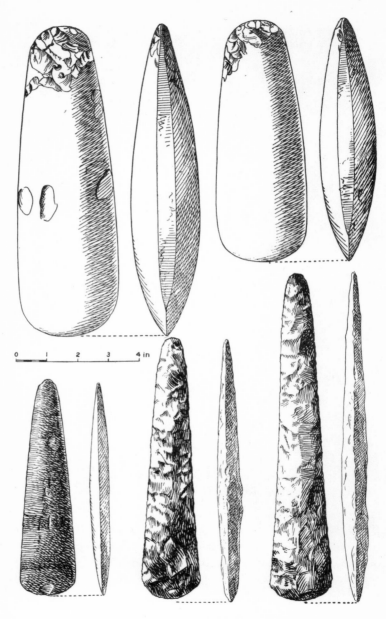

Fig. 28 Bexley Heath, Kent. Hoard of flint axes. Length bottom right 11 ins

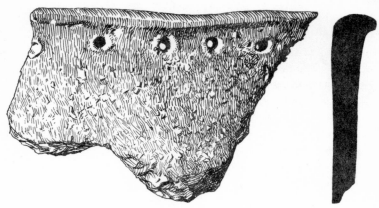

Fig. 29   Grovehurst settlement, Kent. Potsherd with perforations below rim. Possibly 'Western Neolithic'

The perforations can certainly be matched on Windmill Hill wares, but the flint sickles, the plano-convex knives, the arrow-heads and the greenstone axes would all be at home in secondary cultural groups. It must be observed that none of these important Grovehurst discoveries was made in a controlled archaeological excavation. That they were made at all is due to the pit foreman who 'displayed an enthusiastic zeal in the cause, rarely to be met with'.

The paucity of structural evidence of living-places hitherto common throughout Britain is now being redressed but up to the present the south-eastern region has produced nothing like the D-shaped hut foundations associated with Peterborough pottery at Little Paxton, Huntingdonshire, the occupation evidence associated with Windmill Hill pottery and flint-work in the causewayed enclosure at Staines, Middlesex, the evidence from the unusual causewayed enclosure at Lawford in north-east Essex with its Peterborough-type pottery, the rectangular post-built houses at Haldon, Devon, or the timber hut in the forecourt of Sales Lot, Gloucestershire, to name but a few of the major sites which have been examined within recent years.

Casual discoveries of flint implements and pottery, of which there are very many in south-east England, and of the rare and enigmatic pottery spoons of which three are known, do little at present to resolve the relative chronology of early settlement and the direction and extent of secondary influences. They do, however, emphasise the wide geographical distribution of Neolithic settlement on the coast, on downland and along river-courses, and point to the arrival of Beaker-using people who with their knowledge of metalwork and a novel practice of individual inhumation burial, were to bring new ideas to supplement continuing native tradition. Of especial interest in this connection is the remarkable quality of 'Western' sherds found in a store-pit at Wingham, Kent, in 1955, which rank among the finest in Britain. It is not beyond hope that industrial workings or air photography may one day help to provide evidence in the south-east of the long continuity of ritual and ceremonial which at Avebury and Stonehenge extended through many successive changes in material culture.

Plate 16

CHAPTER V

Megalith Builders

IN SOUTH-EAST England remains of prehistoric chamber-tombs exist only in Kent where there are five certain examples, another two which are fairly certain although one was destroyed in the nineteenth century, and several doubtful sites the authenticity of which is based partly on tradition. They lie in two groups east and west of the Medway in its gap through the North Downs, almost at the narrowest point and within shelter of the escarpment.

Fig. 30

This region had many geographical advantages among which were shelter at a moderate height, an abundant water-supply in the streams thrown out at the junction of the Gault Clay with the overlying Chalk, and freedom from dense vegetation. Not the least advantage to the builders of megalithic tombs was a ready supply of natural sarsen stone boulders in such size and form as could easily be moved by rollers and sleds. Both groups, but particularly that on the east, had good access to the River Medway, where a natural crossing at Aylesford, one of the lowest fords on the river, was of the greatest importance from Neolithic times until well into the Middle Ages. In turn the Medway, fully tidal and navigable without difficulty, gave easy access from the estuary of the Thames and so from the sea. There was also good landward communication, for the North Downs Trackway here familiarly known as the Pilgrims Way passes through the western group and, wherever its precise crossing of the Medway may have been, very close to the eastern group.

Tradition and Saxon legend has attached itself to Kits Coty, one of the best known megaliths in Britain, at least since the days of the Elizabethan antiquaries. There are no early forms of the name preserved and the first use of 'Citscote House' was in 1576 by William Lambarde in his *Perambulation of Kent*. The long-accepted popular story of the Hut of Christopher has recently been discussed by Mr John H. Evans in his detailed investigation of the supposed tomb of Horsa the sea-king: origins and meanings he rightly reminds us in this connection are problems to which many antiquaries have been too ready to give too many answers. It may also be said that the White Horse standard first attributed to the invading Saxons by Richard Verstegan in 1634 in his *Restitution of Decayed Intelligence in Antiquities*, legends of which have become attached to more than one of the Kentish megaliths, has no connection at all with the familiar rampant White Horse of Kent which did not appear as a county badge until the early years of the seventeenth century. To return for a moment to the Elizabethan topographers, we note that Camden in the 1586 edition of his *Britannia* wrote of Catigern, son of Vortimer, who fell in single cambat with Horsa:

> (He) was buried in great state, as it is thought, near Ailesford, where those four vast stones are pitched on end, with others lying cross-ways upon them . . . and this the common people do still from Catigern call Keith-coty-house.

Six years earlier John Stow had these straightforward words to say in his *Chronicles of England*:

> Cits cotihous is of foure flat stones, one of them standing up-right in the middle of 2 other, inclosing the edge sides of the first and fourth layd flat aloft the other three; . . . menne may stand on eyther side of the middle stone in tyme of storme or tempest, safe from wind and rayne . . .

Later topographers and historians of note, among them Richard Kilburne in 1659 and John Thorpe in 1788, followed the Cam-den tradition as did Pepys when he recorded in his Diary for 1669 the words paraphrased by a multitude of visitors since:

> But certainly it is a thing of great antiquity and I am mightily glad to see it.

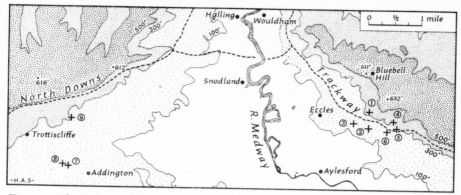

Fig. 30   The Kent megaliths. 1, Kits Coty; 2, Lower Kits Coty; 3, The Coffin Stone; 4, Smythe's Megalith; 5, Upper White Horse Stone; 6, Site of Lower White Horse Stone; 7, Addington Long Barrow; 8, Chestnuts; 9, Coldrum

In the late seventeenth century Druidic legends became firmly attached to several of the megaliths, especially to Kits Coty, and even now they are not entirely forgotten. Stories of warriors and fatal battles associated with the Coffin Stone and the General's Tombstone at Aylesford, the Warrior's Grave at Battle Street, Cobham—though the idea of this non-existent megalith is perpetuated by a small folly megalith in Lady Darnley's Pleasure Garden at Cobham Hall—and stories of bones and armour under Lower Kits Coty may derive from country folk who found it difficult to think that the dead were buried elsewhere than in a churchyard except in time of war. The story told of Lower Kits Coty, popularly known as the Countless Stones, and the baker whose efforts to count them by placing a loaf on each were frustrated by the Devil, is also told of other megaliths notably the Rollright Stones in Oxfordshire. To have done with legend, we mention that the Countless Stones also bore a reputation for assistance to childless women, and that they were regarded with awe not unmixed with a degree of fear well within living memory.

Only one monument, the Chestnuts tomb at Addington, has been excavated with modern technique and method. Coldrum, also in the western group, was last dug at some forty years ago. For the rest, including the whole of the eastern group, apart from recent field-work by Mr Alan McCrerie there is little more than stories of casual discoveries by farmers and antiquarian treasure-hunters. The very large body of older literature dealing with the tombs was summarized in 1924 by O. G. S. Crawford in what became the standard study of its kind.

THE EASTERN GROUP

All are within a short distance of one another in the parish of Aylesford.

KITS COTY

Plate 22

Fig. 31

Kits Coty is a long barrow lying approximately east-west, its outstanding feature being an H-shaped megalithic structure one stone of which stands 8 feet in height, with a massive capstone measuring 12 feet 10 inches by 9 feet 3 inches. A prospect published by Stukeley in 1722 shows a long low mound associated with the megalith and near its far end an isolated recumbent stone called The General's Tomb. The mound is now almost obliterated by ploughing but it can be faintly seen for a distance of some 180 feet; late in the eighteenth century it was a broad ridge lying east/west with the chamber at the eastern end, and the western end bounded by a single large stone, almost certainly the General's Tombstone which was blown to pieces in 1867 as it was an obstacle to ploughing. What may well be a piece of this great stone was uncovered in 1956. The site has been dug into more than once. James Douglas could not find the 'sepulchre' in 1773 but noted in his usually observant way that the soil had been previously disturbed, and in 1854 the enterprising antiquary Thomas Wright who was visiting the district recorded the finding of 'rude pottery' under the monument. In 1940 when the field was under winter wheat part of the outline of the barrow was clearly visible from the air, as were two soil-smears one on each side of the mound nearer to the eastern end than the west. These

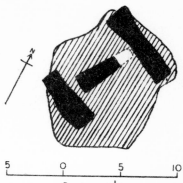

Fig. 31   Kits Coty, Aylesford, Kent. The Chamber

Feet 5 0 5 10

Scale $\frac{1}{100}$

may mark the site of Douglas's excavation or may possibly be the
sites of dug-out side-chambers. One large stone of a revetment was
pulled out from the northern area of the barrow in 1947 and
others are said to remain buried. Recent small-scale digging revealed a deep ditch into which material from the mound was
apparently shovelled when the field was being levelled for
agricultural use.

There is one piece of information recorded by Stukeley in his
Diaries which should not be overlooked in any assessment of the
significance of Kits Coty: in 1723 a correspondent told him that
extending from the north-west and south-east of the stone
chamber there was once 'a parcell of small stones' set in the form
of an arc. That the stones had disappeared by the time of Stukeley's
visit is not at all surprising for local farmers have always been
anxious to break and remove the sarsens which obstructed their
arable fields. As late as Fergusson's visit undertaken for the
preparation of his *Rude Stone Monuments*, 1872, an Aylesford
stonemason thus found full-time employment. Was the 'parcell
of stones' the remains of a forecourt façade at the east end of the
mound? It seems quite likely, and the existing megalithic structure
would then be better regarded as the western, inner, end of a
terminal rectangular chamber and not as a false portal as has
sometimes been suggested. The evidence of stone revetments,

such as it is, would then fall into proper place. Kits Coty may well have had more features in common with Coldrum, Adding-ton and the Chestnuts than at one time seemed likely, but it is idle to speculate until its full story has been elucidated by a methodical excavation.

COUNTLESS STONES
Plate 24

Lower Kits Coty or the Countless Stones, sometimes known as Little Kits Coty, is a confused group of twenty or twenty-one tilted or fallen stones about 500 yards south of Kits Coty. It is impossible to trace the form of the original structure but indications of a mound (and not plough-baulks) were visible some 40 years ago. Douglas was told on good authority in 1773 that a farmer had thrown down the monument to sell its stone as road-metal but the stones were too large and their transport too costly for his purpose. The structure was further damaged on more than one occasion. Stukeley published in 1722 a reconstruction based at third-hand on information from someone who remembered it standing. For what it is worth it shows a structure like a burial-chamber with a D-shaped enclosure of large stones, the chamber being in the middle of the vertical line and projecting on either side of it, rather like the plan of Coldrum which was not known to Stukeley. Stukeley also made a 'ground plot'. It does not agree in detail with his perspective drawings, but it is borne out by a plan which appeared in 1824 when the stones were less confused than they are now, and the fact that his reconstruction has similarities with Coldrum, a monument which he did not know, can be cited in its favour. Its further similarities with another local megalith are noted below.

In this group there are also one or two other sites of interest.

THE COFFIN STONE

The Coffin Stone is a massive recumbent sarsen block 14 feet 6 inches long which lies in a field close to Great Tottington Farm, a quarter of a mile west of Lower Kits Coty. There are two smaller stones near by and there is some evidence that there were formerly two large stones. Human remains including two skulls found under the Coffin Stone in 1836 gave it its name. In all probability the group was once part of a burial-chamber. A short distance away in a picturesque landscape is Tottington spring-head, and here may be seen a group of sarsen stones in great disorder, some being half buried in the stream. The spring water may well have been available to the megalith builders, but neither here nor at Cossington beyond Lower Kits Coty, where there was also a group of sarsens round a spring-head, is it possible to define the site of a monument.

Thanks to the research of Mr John H. Evans following that of O. G. S. Crawford we now have in an accessible form particulars of a megalithic structure uncovered in 1823 by ploughmen working in a field on Warren Farm close to Kits Coty. This sizeable monument, now known as Smythe's Megalith from the Kentish antiquary who made the most reliable contemporary manuscript record of its discovery, consisted of a single 7 foot-long chamber of three large sarsen blocks with a medial slab and pavement and contained human bones together with a piece of an urn of red unglazed pottery, all of which are lost. Some of the eight different accounts of the discovery mention a capstone. Two further stones were found during ploughing in 1965 and one, removed from its hole, may now be seen set in a low ploughed-out east/west mound. Possibly they may indicate the site of another burial chamber. The monument as it is recorded has affinities with the reconstruction plan of its neighbour Lower Kits Coty, with Coldrum and with the recently excavated Chestnuts megalith both of which are important members of the group west of the Medway, and not least is this so in the eastward opening of the burial-chamber.

SMYTHE'S
MEGALITH

In the same field is a notable sarsen block about 8 feet in length and 5 feet in height with fragments of others near it, which may

UPPER
WHITE HORSE
STONE

represent the ruined remains of another burial-chamber. The large stone known as the Upper White Horse Stone (or the Western Sphinx) was once thought by local antiquaries to resemble a horse, as indeed it does, but stories of the god-like White Horse of Kent attached to it are quite without foundation.

Plate 23

LOWER
WHITE HORSE
STONE

Near by is the site of the Lower White Horse Stone (or the Kentish Standard Stone) which was destroyed in 1823. Much nonsense has been written about its supposed association with Kits Coty and the standard of the Saxons.

Sarsen stone boulders are a local geological product resulting from a differential hardening of the Tertiary beds which formerly covered the chalk by infiltration of iron and silica salts in solution. Long after the softer sands had been denuded the harder masses remained stranded on the chalk plateau, tending in the course of time to gather near the escarpment where they are to be found in large numbers on both sides of the Medway Gap. In the Aylesford area alone almost two hundred have been recorded. Much caution is necessary in considering such stones either singly or in groups in this region where known megalithic structures are well represented. It is of course possible that some of the stones may have had a place in prehistoric religious practices, and it is interesting to note that sarsens are sometimes to be seen in or near the fabric of local churches of ancient foundation as at Cobham, Maplescombe, Meopham and Trottiscliffe. Many generations of farmers have broken the stones, dragged them to the edges of fields and banks of streams, used them as road material, stepping-stones for stiles and as stream culverts, even dropping them into convenient hollows as at Cock Adam Shaw, Harvel, which not many years ago was claimed as an important megalith. The so-called Sacred Avenue at Coldrum is nothing more than a farmer's clearance. The great number of sarsens on Bluebell Hill, in Westfield Wood and further eastward at the foot of the Downs, have no known prehistoric associations.

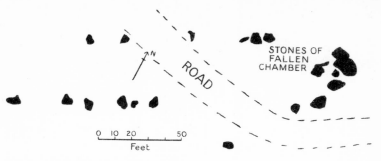

STONES OF
FALLEN
CHAMBER

ROAD

0 10 20   50
Feet

Fig. 32   Addington, Kent. Long barrow

THE WESTERN GROUP

Three megalithic structures of great interest are to be seen in the adjoining parishes of Addington and Trottiscliffe close to the foot of the North Downs on the western side of the Medway.

The Addington long barrow on the Lower Greensand is rectangular in plan and lies north-east/south-west. The scattered members of its sarsen stone revetment form two irregular but almost parallel lines giving an approximate length of 200 feet and a width of some 35 feet. The mound is divided and damaged by a long-existent road and the tumbled stones at its north-east end, now mostly overgrown, are probably those of a burial chamber which was excavated in 1845 by a local parson and subsequently collapsed. A few pieces of rough pottery came from the excavation and there is some, though not very satisfactory, evidence that 'Neolithic sherds' were found by F. J. Bennett, one of the Ightham Circle of archaeologists, in the early years of the present century. The first Treasurer of the Society of Antiquaries, Josiah Colebrooke, visited the monument in 1754 and again in 1761 and left a useful contemporary description and a plan of stones located 'when I thrust my cane into the ground'. Until the barrow is at least cleared, little can be said of its form, its significance in the Medway group, and of a possible comparison with

ADDINGTON
LONG
BARROW
Plate 29
Fig. 32

Kits Coty which was first suggested in 1880 by Flinders Petrie. Indeed it is now impossible to locate the 24 stones which could be traced only forty years ago, while photographs taken in 1906 might be those of another monument, so much has its appearance altered in the meantime.

CHESTNUTS Chestnuts or Stony Warren, a short distance north-westward of the Addington long barrow, had been known since the eighteenth century as a tumbled and confused mass of sarsen stones. The Kentish historian John Harris writing in 1719 saw them as seats for country picnics and it was left to Josiah Colebrooke, on his visits to Addington already noted, to create a Temple of the Ancient Britons. There was little serious doubt that the sixteen or so stones once formed part of a burial-chamber, though whether it formed part of a long barrow as Crawford thought, or of a round barrow, could not be said in the total absence of evidence.

Plates 27, 28

Fig. 33

So it remained until 1957 when, at the initiative and cost of the landowner Mr Richard Boyle and with the co-operation of the Ancient Monuments Department of the then Ministry of Works, the site was carefully excavated and studied by Dr John Alexander. The monument has since been restored and the finds generously presented to Maidstone Museum.

From Dr Alexander's study it became clear that the history of the site fell into four periods. The Addington greensand region as a whole found favour in Mesolithic times, and here in particular there was good evidence that a Mesolithic group had camped and knapped their flints. Some time later a Neolithic community built a megalithic tomb which continued in use in the Early Bronze Age. There was a scatter of Roman material, and in the fourth century a field-hut on the edge of the prehistoric mound was occupied from time to time probably by farm-workers from the extensive settlement on the banks of the Medway at Snodland. Then, in the thirteenth century, the monument was thoroughly and systematically robbed with a purpose which

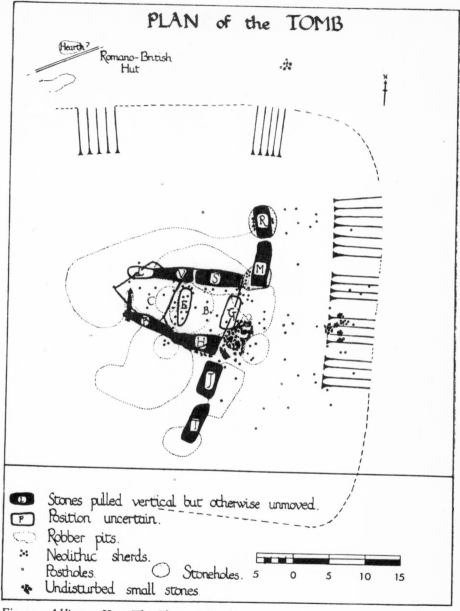

PLAN of the TOMB

Hearth?
Romano-British
Hut

N

R
M
L
V
S
C
B
B
G
F
H
J
I

Stones pulled vertical but otherwise unmoved.
Position uncertain.
Robber pits.
Neolithic sherds.
Postholes.   Stoneholes.
Undisturbed small stones.

5   0   5   10   15

Fig. 33   Addington, Kent. The Chestnuts Tomb

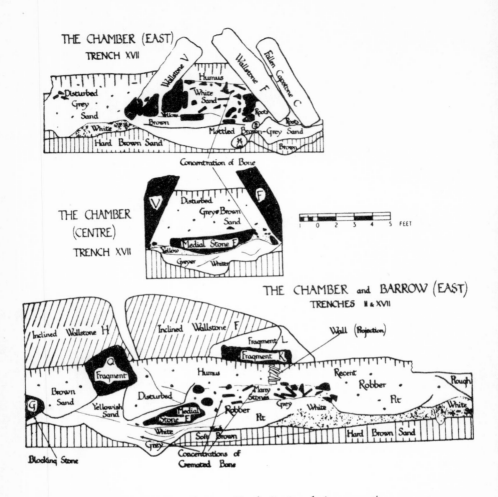

Fig. 34 *Addington, Kent. The Chestnuts Tomb. Sections during excavation*

suggests Royal licence. Its subsequent collapse fortunately sealed telling archaeological evidence which was not disturbed by later treasure-hunters and picnic parties. The interpretation of its stratigraphy was a notable example of modern archaeology in the field.

The original monument was a large barrow with a massive sarsen stone burial-chamber and façade from the undisturbed forecourt of which, as well as from the mediaeval robbers' pits and dumps, were excavated remains of burials with Neolithic-Early Bronze Age relics. The chamber, about 12 feet long, 7½ feet wide and some 10 feet in height, consisted of two trilithons ranged almost due east and west, blocked at each end and by a medial stone. The sarsens which were perhaps chosen for their convenient shape and flat sides were raised directly on the firm underlying sand and supported by blocks of local greensand stone which were used also for the western blocking wall, for a pavement inside the chamber and in the forecourt. Pits were dug for the erection of two stones only, two of the four façade stones, and the holes made by timber stakes used to lever one into position still remained. No trace of the barrow existed above ground and indeed no more than 2 feet of its vertical structure was preserved under the soil. It was D-shaped or trapezoid in plan, about 64 feet in maximum width, about 50 feet in length, and made of scraped-up topsoil. There was no trace of a ditch or a stone peristalith. The barrow, it seems, was raised and then used as a ramp for the erection of the stones, the burial-chamber being temporarily filled with sand which was cleared when the monument was completed. After a sequence of burials the chamber was finally blocked and sealed. This well-informed speculation is certainly welcome in the absence of reliable information from any other of the Kentish megaliths.

Fig. 34

The excavation yielded fragmentary cremated remains of at least nine individuals and one or two infants. Here it should be observed that uncremated bone—there were two unburnt teeth—would have disappeared in the acid sandy soil. The remains appear to have been originally deposited in the eastern part of the chamber with pots of Windmill Hill ware which were later thrown out into the forecourt to be replaced by further burials accompanied by rusticated wares of the Late Neolithic and

Early Bronze Age. The tomb was evidently in use over a long period. Three barbed and tanged flint arrowheads, one leaf-shaped, one petit-tranchet derivative, all fine pieces, and a small holed pendant of baked clay complete the list of grave-goods. All would be at home in a western Neolithic-Early Bronze Age context.

COLDRUM

Plates 25, 26

Fig. 35

Fig. 36

Coldrum in Trottiscliffe parish apparently takes its unusual name from the near-by farm-house Coldrum Lodge which was built in 1796. No earlier forms of the name are known. The monument is a rectangular mound about 70 feet long and 55 feet broad orientated east/west with a revetment of sarsen orthostats, some of which are fallen, and a rectangular burial-chamber of four massive sarsens at its east end. It stands in a commanding position on the lower slopes of the chalk hills and on the edge of a natural terrace so that the burial-chamber is now some 17 feet above the level of the ground below. Twenty-four stones of a peristalith lie on the terrace in their approximate original positions, while 17 have fallen on to the slope and to the foot of the terrace. Some of the many writers on Coldrum have thought that the monument thus lies on two levels or that the burial-chamber once stood inside a circle of stones, but recent study by Mr John H. Evans shows conclusively that the burial-chamber lay at the east end of the monument and that the 17 stones have fallen from their original positions as part of the peristalith. As late as 1908 there was a medial stone in the burial-chamber, and a drawing made some sixteen years earlier by a reliable antiquary shows that it had a half-round perforation not unlike a port-hole entrance.

The monument has suffered badly. It was once a farmyard rubbish tip and chalk-hole, and part of its collapse was due to digging by local people who were trying to find a supposed underground passage to the village church. There are various stories of human bones being found in the chamber and on the slope below. 'Saxon' Kemble dug here about 1856 and with no

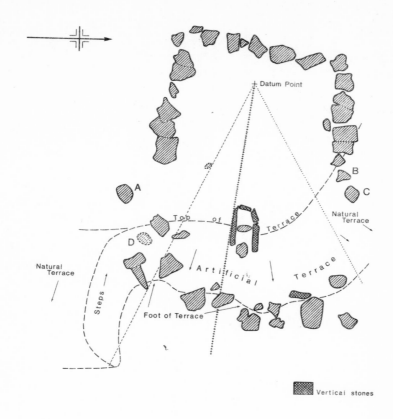

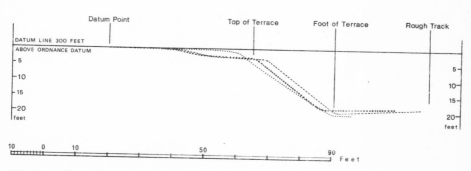

Datum Point

A

B

C

Natural
Terrace

Top   of   Terrace

D

Natural
Terrace

Steps

Artificial   Terrace

Foot of Terrace

Vertical stones

Datum Point

Top of Terrace

Foot of Terrace

Rough Track

DATUM LINE 300 FEET
ABOVE ORDNANCE DATUM

5

10

15

20
feet

5

10

15

20
feet

10   0   10

50

90
Feet

Figs. 35, 36   Coldrum, Trottescliffe, Kent. Plan and sections

109

surprise found pottery 'undoubtedly of Saxon manufacture'. The published results of an organised excavation in 1910 by F. J. Bennett may be quickly summarised. The bones of some 22 individuals of both sexes and widely-spread ages were found on two stone pavements within the north-west part of the chamber, one skull being supported by two blocks of local ironstone, while 'close by was a flint saw and small portions of rude pottery'.

Nothing remains but a small rim sherd of 'Western Neolithic' pottery in Maidstone Museum, a collection of post-cranial bones in the British Museum (Natural History) and a few in the Duck-worth Laboratory at Cambridge, this skeletal material having escaped the destruction of the greater part by war-time enemy action. There is some welcome anatomical detail. Many bones were deliberately broken, perhaps after intentional exposure or temporary burial in a mortuary-house, and in this collective burial-place as in the Lanhill, Wiltshire long barrow, many showed common family traits. These people were long-headed and short in stature, we are told, good-looking and of moderate muscular strength with wide feet free in movement; they had healthy teeth with an edge-to-edge bite, the aged suffered from rheumatism which was not helped by the constant squatting posture deduced from a characteristic flattening of their shin-bones. In spite of all this, we know next to nothing of material possessions, nothing of daily life and its relative chronology except on the basis of wide analogy.

The site was cleared of undergrowth, fallen stones underpinned, and dug at again in 1922, 1923 and 1926 when the burial-chamber was re-opened and excavations made at the base of its stones, but no adequate report was published. References to trenches under stones of the burial-chamber and to human bones found there are far from clear. The monument is now a memorial to Benjamin Harrison, the Kentish prehistorian, and in the care of the National Trust; the Postmaster General has played his part by naming a new local telephone exchange as

Coldrum Stones. Finally it is well to recall that Coldrum is a structure on its own and not associated with any alignment or stone avenue as has sometimes been claimed.

The excavation of Chestnuts and recent study by Mr John H. Evans have now made possible some reconsideration of the nature and origins of the Medway megaliths, but the fascinating problem of their precise significance in a wider archaeological context is far from solved. We do well to remind ourselves at once that there has been but one skilled and satisfactory excavation, and not a single absolute date.

Some time ago and largely on the evidence of geographical distribution and older plans Professor Stuart Piggott had pointed out that there were seemingly similar structures in Holland, while Dr Glyn Daniel urged the possibility of an origin in Scandinavia. But tombs in those areas appear to lack the one constant characteristic of the Medway Group, namely the burial-chamber at the east end, and while there is good archaeological evidence of a Kentish connection with Scandinavia in Neolithic times, it is not to be associated particularly with the megaliths. Further, the results of Dr Alexander's excavation of Chestnuts do not in any way support an origin from across the North Sea although his rusticated pottery (generally referred to as 'Secondary' Neolithic) could indicate a later trading connection with the Low Countries. The tomb-plan, the cremation burial rite and the associated grave-goods point rather to the Cotswolds and perhaps Wessex, a view which was put forward on other grounds nearly fifty years ago by O. G. S. Crawford in his discerning study of the Kentish long barrows and megaliths. That there are no known tombs of this kind in the countryside between Kent and Berkshire need not detract from the merit of these views.

At the same time the all-important geographical feature of access by sea and river and all that it implies must again be emphasised and particularly so since megaliths in Dorset, in the Channel Island of Guernsey and on the French coast of the

Channel have features related to those of the Chestnuts monu﹍ment. Some of the Channel tombs were almost certainly derived in their turn from Ireland and the east of Scotland, as both Dr Glyn Daniel and Professor Stuart Piggott have pointed out, and it may not be accidental that the best parallels to the Chestnuts are in Northern Ireland. In this connection the large quantity of Irish Bronze Age gold found on the coasts and waterways of Kent is also worth noting.

In summary, then, the Medway megaliths may at present be regarded as an outlier of the large and familiar complex of the Atlantic coast with some influence from the Low Countries and with an ultimate western origin in Ireland or Brittany. It could indeed be, as Dr Alexander hints, that they form an isolated pocket of the Clyde﹍Carlingford culture. What is certain at Addington at least, is that local Neolithic traditions and trading connections continued into the Early Bronze Age without any cultural break.

The time for morphological study is surely now past. Only further excavation can answer the questions we really wish to ask, but meanwhile Dr Colin Renfrew's 'Colonialism and Megalithismus' and Dr Glyn Daniel's 'Northmen and South﹍men' provide a salutary background discipline.

At the same time, as Glyn Daniel reminds us, the closest parallels to Coldrum are the *dysser* of Denmark, and some of the Medway tombs may well be members of the *dös/dysse* class of the Danish Neolithic. His questions of 'Where?, How?, Why?, and When?' can scarcely be answered without reference, in the Medway area, to the sea﹍way of the English Channel.

CHAPTER VI

Early Traders in Metal

THE PRESENCE OF the familiar beaker-type pottery—
drinking cups for milk or beer—in a store-pit overlying the
Neolithic levels in the causewayed enclosure at Whitehawk and
of beakers in the filling of two Sussex flint mines is only part of
evidence more strongly exhibited elsewhere in Britain that the
Beaker Peoples in their widespread search for sources of metal
overlapped the cultures of the later Neolithic farmers. In the south-
east a few beakers are associated with simple copper and bronze
daggers and knives, and whether these were obtained by war or,
as seems much more likely, by trade from Wessex or Ireland,
they are the earliest known objects of metal and it is with a note
on the beaker-using peoples that this chapter must commence.

BEAKER PEOPLES

The main areas of settlement known from burials and stray
discoveries are in East Kent, along the Thames, the Medway and
on the South Downs. Among the intrusive groups and later
native developments spread between about 2000 and 1700 BC
are varieties of European bell-beakers, beakers with immediate
affinities in the Middle Rhine and the Low Countries and
eventually of a Southern British and an East Anglian tradition.

The main groups of beakers, A, B and C, have often been
studied on a chronological and cultural basis. In Sussex the basis
of a detailed analysis of fabric and decoration was laid down in
1954 by Mr R. C. Musson. No other county has been so well
served but the application of such methods must be extended
beyond artificial local boundaries if it is to be effective. Modern
application of delicate and accurate analysis can best be accom-
plished, as Dr D. L. Clarke showed in 1962, with the skilled
aid of an electronic brain. Some idea of the scope of his enquiry

becomes evident when he says that beaker pottery in general has a minimum of 39 variable qualities, and the matrix when sorted must of course be considered with all other aspects of beaker culture. It is possible that Dr Clarke's forthcoming major work will throw a new light on many of these aspects. Meanwhile it may be said that B-type beakers are restricted in their distribution to the south-east, a region almost devoid of A and C types and, apart from the trade traffic area of the Thames, almost equally devoid of the flint daggers associated elsewhere with A and C beakers. Many of the finds, especially those in Sussex, reflect the attention of collectors and there are very few from closed archaeo-logical contexts. One of the latter will be noted when the Late Bronze Age urnfield on Steyning Round Hill is considered.

Plate 30

Only here and there it is possible to see a little beyond the relics. A contracted skeleton at Falmer, Sussex, with a B-type beaker at its feet had a barbed and tanged arrowhead under the skull and a pile of snail shells deliberately placed before the mouth. In a barrow at Beggars Haven near Devils Dyke, also on the South Downs, a girl had been buried in a contracted position with her necklace of lignite and tubular bronze beads. At Sittingbourne, Kent, a warrior was buried with his tanged and riveted bronze knife, bowman's wrist-guard and bone belt-hook. The com-posite bowl-barrow, Money Mound, excavated in 1961 by Mr S. G. Beckensall provided fragments of an A-type beaker identified partly on the basis of matrix analysis and a barbed and tanged arrowhead, although the primary burial had disappeared and there was much subsequent disturbance particularly in Roman times when the site was a votive shrine over more than three centuries. A most interesting feature of this barrow was the filling of hard white local 'silt' between the two roughly concen-tric rings of sandstone, a contrast perhaps to the gleaming white chalk of the downland barrows.

Plate 31

When we turn to living-places we find a great paucity of satis-factory evidence. The small pit with the ashes of a hearth containing beaker fragments above the Neolithic occupation at Whitehawk is about the sum of it in the south-east and we must look elsewhere in Britain for details of the domestic life of these agriculturists who grew flax and barley and reared cattle, sheep and pigs.

EARLY BARROW-CEMETERIES

Here in the south-east there are no sacred sites, no 'Henge' monuments to mark with additions to their structures the wealth and importance of the middlemen who were concerned in advances in metallurgy, the practice of agriculture and the prosecution of overseas trade with Central Europe which brought indirect contact with the Eastern Mediterranean. Such sites could easily have been destroyed without recognition in urban and industrial development and others may remain for future discovery. In the present state of knowledge the early and middle parts of the Bronze Age are represented almost solely by a very large number of burial-mounds. Dwelling-places are not known and of the barrows only two have been excavated with modern method. It is unfortunate that one of the latter, a fine bell-barrow in Deerleap Wood, Wotton, Surrey, provided no direct evidence of its date. Remarkable barrow-cemeteries, among which are seven barrows on Reigate Heath, Surrey, four bowl-barrows at West End Common and three bell-barrows enclosed within a single ditch at Elstead, all in the same county, no less than 50 bowl-barrows near Firle Beacon, ten on Heyshott Downs, the six great bell-barrows called the Devil's Jumps on Treyford Hill, the four Devil's Humps at Bow Hill and the well-preserved barrows at Kingley Vale, all in Sussex, as well as small groups at Ringwould and Brockman's Bushes in East Kent provide some idea of the extent and nature of the settlement of a pastoral aristocracy which had connections with the Wessex middlemen traders centred on the region of Stonehenge. East Kent, as Messrs Paul Ashbee and G. C. Dunning have emphasised in a recent study

Plate 35

of the round barrows in that region, lies athwart the presumed trading routes linking Wessex with the Low Countries and the northern Rhineland, and acceptable evidence from the contents of these barrows and of others from the South Downs of Sussex points to a southern coastal route in addition to one by the Thames Estuary. Several barrows are worth special notice.

A barrow at Hove, Sussex—it is the only one on the coastal plain—destroyed in 1857 is of sufficient importance to have gained a place in international literature. Within a 6 foot-long oak coffin was a handled cup turned from a block of red amber, a stone battle-axe perforated for hafting, a grooved bronze dagger with remains of its leather-lined wooden sheath and a small whet-stone which was worn on the belt. The barrow was a large one, 12 feet in height and perhaps about 200 feet in diameter, and the presence of such a rarity as the amber cup, one of the most remarkable prehistoric antiquities ever found in Britain, and of the fine ceremonial battle-axe, suggests the burial of a highly individual chieftain with Baltic and Scandinavian connections and, as his characteristic dagger shows, a contact also with the culture of Wessex. Is it possible that the amber cup was on its way to be traded for Irish or Welsh gold by way of a Wessex merchant middleman?

Plate 32

On the edge of the Channel shore are two bowl-barrows on the chalk cliffs at Ringwould, Kent, which were excavated in 1872 with some care. The account is illustrated with plans and sections, and with James Douglas's plans of his Saxon barrows excavated on Chatham Lines in 1779 is worthy of note as a remarkable departure from the then contemporary scene of social antiquarianism. One barrow contained no relics. The other, a mound 75 feet in diameter, covered four burial-pits each con-taining a cremation in an inverted urn, an 'incense cup' with one urn, two with another which was also accompanied by a burnt substance and light-green faience beads of Oriental origin. One of the urns is of 'applied horse-shoe' type. Flint nodules piled

Plate 33
Fig. 37

over one burial, sea-shells, and a lump of iron pyrites from the local chalk—still popularly known as fools' gold or thunder-bolts—are in a minor degree a reflection of the richer objects found in Wessex. At Tilmanstone in East Kent a slotted 'incense cup' was found in a barrow with an inhumation burial and another was found near Canterbury. Other pottery evidence of the Wessex culture comes from East Kent barrows at Capel-le-Ferne, Nackington, Westbere and Stodmarsh.

This influence is further exemplified by the contents of several of the Sussex downland barrows which were plundered in the nineteenth century. At Oxteddle Bottom near Lewes an over-hanging-rim cinerary urn contained amber beads, a jet button, a bronze spiral finger-ring, a pendant and a segmented bead of green faience. A blue faience pendant and an 'incense cup' came from a cremation burial in a barrow at Clayton Hill, and at

Fig. 38

Fig. 37 Left, urn from Capel Barrow, Kent, height 13.9 ins; right, urn from Ringwould Barrow, Kent, height 16 ins

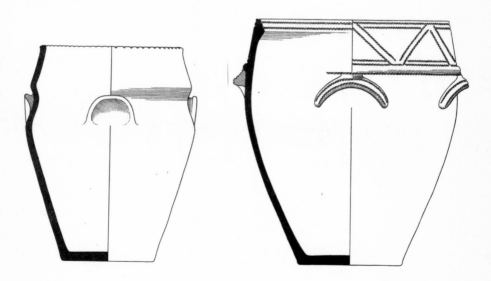

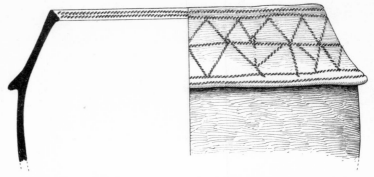

Fig. 38 Oxteddle Bottom, Sussex. Urn with trinkets of amber (A), bronze (Br), faience (F) and jet (unlettered)

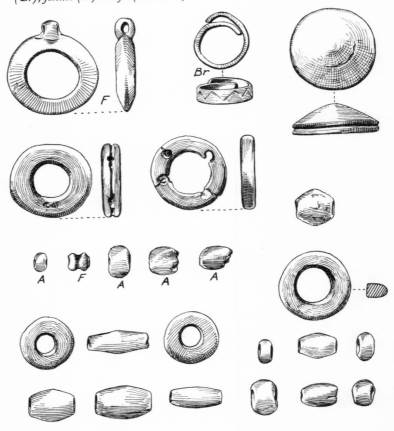

Cliffe Hill, Lewes, a barrow contained amber and jet rings and beads, and beads and a pendant of green faience as well as a bronze ring and a miniature cup. In 1872 Pitt Rivers opened the Black Burgh, south of the Devil's Dyke, and found an 'eyebrow cup', shale beads, a bronze pin and, perhaps curiously in a woman's inhumation, a riveted and ribbed bronze dagger. Whether the little cup came from the Aegean or from the southern Baltic is not certain.

In the early metropolis of Wessex a powerful religious belief was centred upon Stonehenge; in the south-east between about 1600 and 1200 BC it was centred on the barrow-cemeteries and the barrows of the aristocracy. It is tempting to see some persistence of folk-memory enshrined in the Good Friday junketings once held around the Hove barrow and in the use of Five Lords' Burgh near Alfriston as the meeting-place of five Sussex parishes of old foundation. A magnificent Wessex bell-barrow, the 'Wen Barrow of Wanborough' by the Hog's Back in Surrey, was, like Money Mound, still visited in Roman times. More recent history is represented by an inscription and flagstaff on a fine bowl-barrow on Puttenham Golf Course in Surrey; a stone records that Queen Victoria used the mound in 1858 as a base from which to review her troops. We can but wonder, too, what came from the 25 barrows noted by Camden at Thunderhill above Addington in 1586, and from the 23 on Wimbledon Common where Stukeley dug about 1760 and James Douglas followed him 20 years later.

THE FOOD-VESSEL CULTURE

Partly contemporary with the Secondary Neolithic and Wessex Cultures was that of a people who are named from their characteristic pottery, the food vessel. In the north and west of Britain these farmers and traders were able to import exotic objects and their way of life flourished. In the south-east they left but little trace. It seems that they owed something to the users of beaker

Plate 34

pottery, but since only five or six examples of food-vessels are recorded, their significance is not clear. A fine example found on the Greensand belt at Abinger Hammer, Surrey, in 1960 and published in detail by Messrs E. S. Wood and N. P. Thompson seems rather to represent an eastern outlier of Wessex Culture; a careful excavation and resistivity tests did not disclose a barrow or any features of structural interest. The plano-convex flint knives often associated with the Food-Vessel Culture also appear in the south-east, particularly in Sussex, but scarcely ever in an archaeological context. Of the daily life of the food-vessel users in the south-east, nothing is known. A small nomadic and pastoral population with a degree of internal trading prosperity seems likely.

In the region of south-east England covered by this book there are records of but eight collared urns in the Primary Series as defined by Dr Ian Longworth, but of many more pots in the Peterborough tradition, especially in Surrey, Kent and the Thames Valley. It may be that a drift of population is indicated, but the evidence is not yet sufficient to allow of more than a suggestion of a perhaps more probable indigenous tradition. No settlements appear to be known.

METAL-WORKING

The development of metallurgy in the south-east during the Middle Bronze Age shows several interesting features. In considering 115 rapiers from the Thames, Mrs Bridget Trump shows

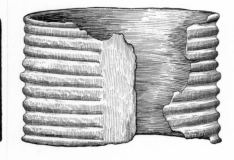

Fig. 39   Ramsgate, Kent. Bronze armlet and, right, bracelets. Diam. of armlet 4.8 ins

fully how the native design of dirks and rapiers differs from that of Contintental prototypes. They are, she says, 'works of art, masterpieces of casting and extremely effective weapons'. The ornament horizon discussed fully by Dr M. A. Smith in a masterly study represents the impact of Nordic continental influences on our domestic industries. Many specifically British products inspired by North European contacts are found in the south-east. The well-known 'Sussex loops', bracelets of cast rod with a backward-bent loop, most of them found within 6 miles of Brighton (though there are two doubtfully found in Surrey and one or two much wider afield, including one in Heathery Burn Cave, Durham) can now be placed in their proper archaeo-logical context. In the often cited Late Middle Bronze Age hoard from Black Rock, Brighton, three were found, with the blade of a dagger, the handle of a bronze dirk, a coiled finger-ring,

Plate *37*

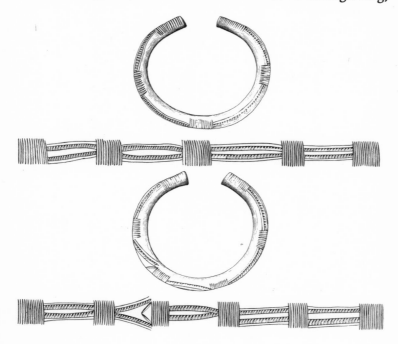

eight flat palstaves and two bronze oval bracelets. On two Sussex sites the loops were associated with quoit-headed bronze pins and again with coiled bronze finger-rings and a British looped bronze spear-head. At Ramsgate, Kent, an inhumation burial in a carefully dug grave in the chalk was accompanied by a bronze ribbed wristlet and two pennanular brooches decorated with a zoned pattern of traced ellipses which was derived from a north-west German source. This decoration is related to that on Professor Christopher Hawkes's 'Picardy' pins, of which four of the five English examples come from the coast of Kent. Three of the pins from Ramsgate were in an urn related to the pottery traditions of the latter part of the Middle Bronze Age and in particular to the 'Drakenstein' series found in the Low Countries.

Fig. 39

THE LATER BRONZE AGE

The south-east has contributed much to our knowledge of Britain in the latter part of the conventional Bronze Age. There was some deterioration in climate but the life of the wandering pastoralists was merged with, and in some areas gave place to, a more settled living based on intensive farming, the use of the ox-drawn plough and the cultivation of large tracts of arable land. In addition, a plentiful supply of bronze brought with it new metal tools and weapons and greatly advanced techniques in metallurgy. New ideas came from the crowded lands of northern and western France, brought by people who were ultimately refugees from Central Europe and whose develop-ment had been affected by the demands for gold, copper and bronze from the Aegean world.

FARMSTEADS

Thanks again to the devoted and skilled field-work of Sussex archaeologists a good deal is known about farming life in the latter part of the Bronze Age. Sites on the South Downs at High Down, excavated in 1869 and 1939, Park Brow in 1924,

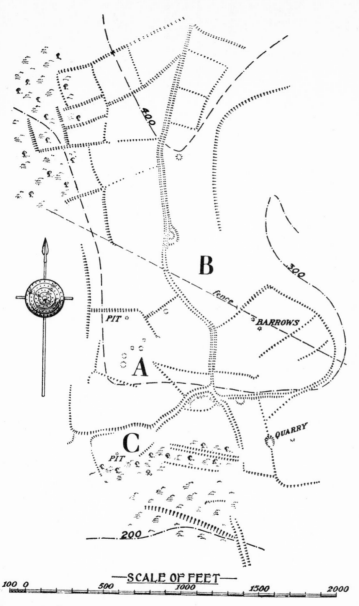

PIT

400

B

300

fence

A

PIT

BARROWS

C

QUARRY

PIT

200

—SCALE OF FEET—

100 0   500   1000   1500   2000

Fig. 40 Park Brow, Sussex. Farmsteads: A Bronze Age, B Iron Age,
C Iron Age and Roman

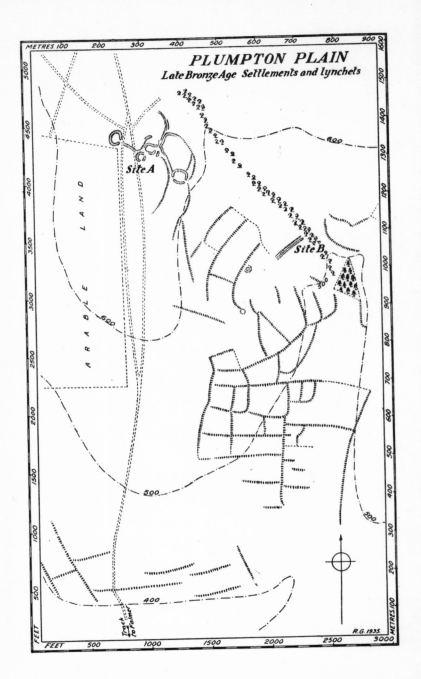

PLUMPTON PLAIN
Late Bronze Age Settlements and lynchets

Site A

Site B

Track to Falmer

R.G. 1935.

New Barn Down in 1933 and Plumpton Plain in 1934, among others, have added to our knowledge, and pottery from these sites and in particular from Plumpton Plain provided the typological and chronological basis for the well-known study made in 1935 by Professor Christopher Hawkes. Views on chronology have since been modified more than once, but there now seems to be a general measure of agreement with Professor Hawkes' original scheme. This matter of chronology will no doubt be considered again when absolute evidence becomes available in future excavations and when an acceptable system of matrix analysis has been evolved.

Fig. 40

Plumpton Plain A on the top of the South Downs was a small farmstead of circular huts with compounds, fields and roadways. The relatively small quantity of pottery and domestic rubbish suggests a temporary occupation. There was one bronze ferrule, and a leaf-shaped arrowhead, a sickle flake, a saw, an axe and scrapers of flint and a couple of whetstones show well enough a traditional native background. Site B on the slope of the hill to which the inhabitants later migrated was marked by a single bank and ditch. Its round huts and storage-pits yielded pottery of Deverel-Rimbury tradition, pottery decorated with hatched triangles reminiscent of West Alpine Hallstatt traditions, a bronze knife and part of a winged Alpine-type axe, spindle-whorls and loom-weights, hammerstones and whetstones but the flint industry was less well marked. Two groups of field-boundary lynchets which may well have formed part of this farming settlement appear to have been destroyed by modern ploughing.

Fig. 41

Of the fifteen or so Late Bronze Age settlements in Sussex none is better known than that on the southern slope of Itford Hill, Beddingham, which was excavated for five seasons beginning in 1949 by Messrs G. P. Burstow and G. A. Holleyman for the Brighton and Hove Archaeological Society. Here was

Fig. 41 Plumpton Plain, Sussex. Bronze Age farmsteads

an enclosed farmstead amid Celtic fields where barley was grown and sheep and oxen raised. This small hamlet of thirteen round plan timber framed huts gave home to a family of some twenty people and it was occupied at the most for a quarter of a century. The main farmstead contained living huts, a weaving shed and storage hut, a cooking area and huts serving as barns, byres and workshops. The largest hut, probably that of the owner, had on the ground level of its inner doorway a large chalk phallus, a symbol of hoped for fertility in flocks and herds. In all, about half a hundredweight of potsherds representing 96 vessels of simple bucket, barrel or bag shape were recovered. They formed a homogeneous group which was put (in 1957) in Late Bronze Age I, 1000–750 BC; an alternative date of 1200–1000 BC has also been suggested. The hut here illustrated in the plan of its post holes had an entrance porch; it housed a primitive loom and later when the hut was rebuilt it contained two storage pits from one of which $11\frac{1}{2}$ lb. of unthreshed carbonised barley was recovered. It is of interest to note that a large storage pit in the settlement at New Barn Down probably held enough cereal to last ten to fifteen people for one year. On the floor were trodden in potsherds, several cylindrical loom weights of baked clay and pieces of Greensand stone saddle querns. The probable appearance of the settlement is shown in Mr Patrick Burke's drawing. No other settlement of its kind has been so well excavated. Its banks and enclosures are still visible and from them can be seen a magnificent panorama of the Ouse Valley and its downland setting.

In some instances the lay out of field systems, boundary dykes and farm roads and trackways has been well preserved. On Fore Down and in Old Kiln Bottom at Lullington, for example, many of these features could still be recognised until a few years ago. Whether they are to be attributed technically to the Bronze Age or the Early Iron Age is a matter of opinion, but such farming patterns probably altered but little over the centuries.

Fig. 42

Fig. 43

Fig. 44

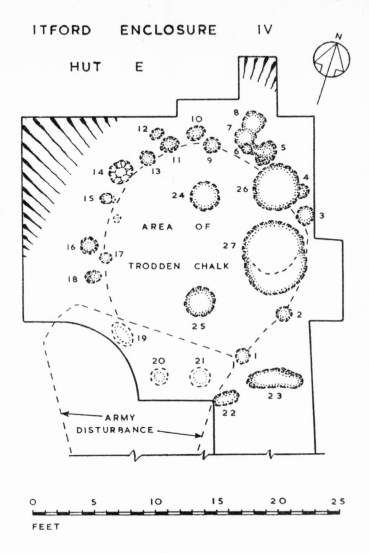

ITFORD ENCLOSURE IV

HUT E

AREA OF

TRODDEN CHALK

ARMY
DISTURBANCE

FEET

Fig. 42 Itford Hill, Sussex. Hut plan

Fig. 43   Itford Hill, Sussex. Probable original appearance

Few settlements are known apart from those on the South
Downs. On the Sussex coastal plain there is evidence of Late
Bronze Age storage pits at Selsey and Kingston Buci and of a
circular hut with a deliberately sanded floor at the centre of a
ring ditch on the Wadhurst Clay at Playden near Rye, close to
which was a wattle fenced rectangular enclosure, perhaps a
cattle pen. One or two sites in East Kent also indicate the
presence of these Late Bronze Age farmers and probably more
await discovery. At Deal, a circular V shaped ditch was exca
vated in 1934; it had a causeway with three post holes on each

side. Fragments of Late Bronze Age pottery came from the ditch and there were also clay daub from a wattle hut and bones of ox, horse, sheep, pig and dog.

An unusual site at Broomwood, St Paul's Cray in north-west Kent, was examined in 1952 by Mr John Parsons in advance of its destruction for the building of a modern church. A rectangular banked enclosure with entrances in its longer sides had two hut-sites at opposed corners. The acid soil had destroyed any possible occupation debris other than flint and no flint-work was excavated *in situ* although much was recovered from the immediate area of one hut and from the hill-top. In general the flint work was of Bronze Age appearance and some of it was described as 'rather late in the Early Bronze Age'. The

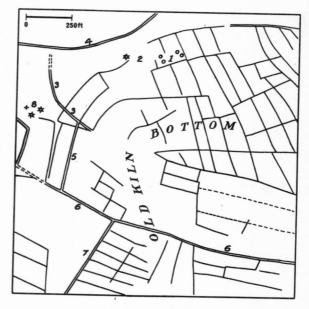

Fig. 44 Old Kiln Bottom, Lullington, Sussex. Celtic field-system: 1 Late Bronze Age–Early Iron Age hut sites preceding field-system; 2 Modern dew-pond; 3 Cross-ridge dyke leading to 4|5 Hollow-ways connected walk; 6 The main field-way contemporary with the field-system; 7 Branch field-ways; 8 Pond barrows

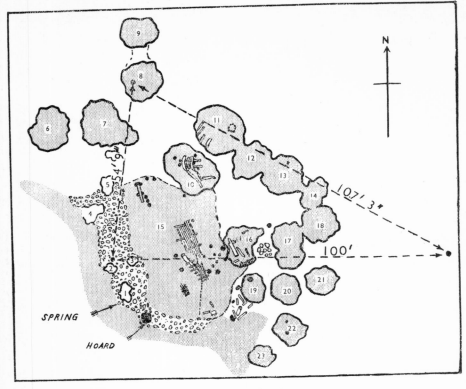

Fig. 45   Minnis Bay, Birchington, Kent. Bronze Age site

so-called 'hut circles' on Hayes Common in the same region of Kent have sometimes been claimed as of Bronze Age date but on no real evidence.

PILE-DWELLINGS

One of the most interesting Late Bronze Age settlements in Britain was exposed during a winter gale in 1938 off the coast of Minnis Bay, Birchington in north-east Kent. It was discovered by G. J. D'A. Beck, a 14-year-old scholar of King's School, Canterbury, whose untimely death less than a year later deprived his county of a promising young archaeologist. The site was covered at high water and such rescue and excavation as could be done over a trying period of two years had to be undertaken between tides. Two stages of occupation were recognised. The first, a large hollow and twenty-three pits, some apparently rush-lined, dug into the natural chalk, was abandoned after flooding; the site was re-occupied later when it had been protected by a timber-laced gravel bank. It was Beck's discovery of a hoard of 73 bronzes under the gravel bank which first drew attention to the site. Botanical analysis of silt from the area reflected the cultivation of crops and the residue of threshing; the earlier pits probably served for storage before they were filled with domestic refuse and occasional human remains. The later occupants raised hazel wattle-work huts on piles over the earlier pits but the havoc of the sea made it almost impossible for the excavators to regain much by way of plan. There was evidence of substantial tree-trunk buildings held together by bonds of withy. Among the pottery, fragmented and in poor state, were sherds of carinated bowls, round-shouldered jars, 'situla' jars and 'sugar-basin' bowls with cable and finger-printed decoration, all typical of Late Bronze Age assemblages. The bronze hoard, with which was a bone point, contained founder's waste, cake metal, personal ornaments, pieces to be applied to leatherwork, bits of swords and spear-heads, 19 socketed axes, 4 winged axes, gouges, chisels and a hammer and sickle. Here on the southern shore of the Thames Estuary are traces of the exotic bronzes of West Alpine immigrants seen more particularly at Old England much further up the river. In the Minnis Bay hoard there was also a piece of the handle of a bronze cauldron. It is one of the few examples found in England; other fragments of cauldrons are known from Sussex, from Ditchling, and more notably from Sompting, the latter from an old and much-worn vessel which might have had a capacity of five gallons. At Sompting, too, were broken sheets from old and larger cauldrons and 17

Fig. 45

socketed axes including several rough castings from the same mould. Such cauldrons of riveted sheet bronze, well represented by an example from the Thames at Battersea, are products of Irish workshops as the discovery of 28 examples in that country demonstrates, and it has been suggested that they were made by family groups, the skill and technique being passed down from father to son. Be this as it may, the southern shore of the Thames Estuary evidently lay on one of the principal trade-routes between Britain and the Continent as it had done in the past and was to continue to do for many centuries in the future.

Plate 36

BURIALS OF THE LATE BRONZE AGE

The first Late Bronze Age urnfield to be discovered in Sussex was found after two schoolboys had in 1949 collected pieces of nine pots and cremated bones from under the plough-soil on Steyning Round Hill. Subsequent investigation showed a circular area about 30 feet in diameter covered with large flints. Fragments of beaker pottery came from a shallow depression and it seems that a beaker burial was covered not by a barrow but by a cairn of flints. This primary burial was surrounded by some 36 burials of the Late Bronze Age; there were four cremations without urns, and possibly others. There was also a collared urn of Middle Bronze Age type and urns technically of Late Bronze Age types. In his account of the excavation Mr G. P. Burstow has emphasised that although this is the first discovery of its sort in Sussex, there are as at Plumpton Plain, Itford Hill, Park Brow, Blackpatch, and New Barn Down habitation sites of the same period. Here again we may see evidence of a continuity in tradition.

Burial mounds of the latter part of the Bronze Age are known at Wonersh, Chobham, Worplesdon and Wimbledon in Surrey. They belonged apparently to groups of nomadic herds-men who travelled the heaths and the countryside of the Wealden greensands though nothing is known at present about their way of life. It may be guessed that in some ways they were influenced by the Wessex people, perhaps also by contact with the very few Food-Vessel people in the area, but almost certainly they owed much to persistent native tradition.

Some years ago the late Dr E. Cecil Curwen drew up an instructive table of the associated implements and hoards then known from his own county of Sussex. From 35 hoards there were records of about 380 tools and weapons of some 24 varieties with an expected preponderance of later types. In geographical distribution they came from the downland, the coastal plain and very occasionally from the heathland in the north of the region. Three or four with cakes of metal, scraps and jets from casting were obviously the stocks and stores of bronze-founders; others with bronzes from the same mould represented the stores of merchant traders, among which the group of 90 palstaves, some worn and fragmentary, of Professor Hawkes' Type B found at Bognor is of especial interest. One founder's hoard from Worthing was in its owner's travelling-pot. A set of six tools, a winged socketed axe, two socketed gouges, a tanged chisel, an awl and a knife found at Newhaven may have belonged to a working carpenter. Further removed from the work-a-day life are four flanged axes, three of them deliberately broken, placed as a votive offering in the Combe Hill barrow at Jevington. A modern typological study of all these bronzes might well produce some surprising conclusions.

In Kent we have already noticed the large and important hoard from Minnis Bay, Birchington, with its West Alpine bronzes. Two hoards come from the river-girt Hundred of Hoo. Another waterside site on the Isle of Harty furnished the large founder's hoard upon which Sir John Evans drew in 1881 for his classic account of bronze-moulding. The 32 pieces found in a drainage trench about 1873 include a tubular toggle reminiscent

Plate 38

of a Hallstatt background besides items from the carp's-tongue sword complex of the Late Bronze Age and a few which may be of earlier date. The very large hoard from Ebbsfleet, Minster-in-Thanet on the Channel coast here illustrated also included tubular toggles and evidently belonged to a founder in a large way of business who was also in contact with West Alpine sources. An interesting hoard of 53 pieces found 20 feet deep in a sand-pit at Bexley Heath, Kent, in 1930 is principally of the Late Bronze Age though some earlier forms are represented; a date of about 700 BC onwards seems to be indicated. A hoard found in 1914 in making a bunker on Addington Golf Course, Surrey, is of the carp's-tongue sword complex.

A hoard of some 13 pieces including a socketed axe, sickle, pins, rings and bracelets found in an 'earthen vessel' at Marden in the Weald of Kent is unusual, but its presence is to be seen against the background of charcoal for fuel and the near-by River Beult rather than of a mysterious secret isolation deep in the forest land.

Many notable bronzes have been recovered from the Thames itself as may be seen in the famous Layton Collection now in the London Museum. Dredging, fishing and other waterside occupations are not normally conducive to the finding and recovery of hoards, and of all the more interest therefore is a collection of 38 spear-heads, a dagger, tanged knife and a trunnioned chisel dredged off Broadness, Swanscombe. The spear-heads included some which were leaf-shaped, some barbed with lunate openings and pin, and one which appears to bear traces of applied gold decoration as does another from the Thames near Battersea.

As a whole the hoards provide evidence of improved weapons, a wider variety of tools for the farmer, carpenter and the bronze-worker himself, of specialised craftsmen and merchants who travelled quite widely on the waterways, and of a people who sometimes broke their bronzes deliberately as part of a ritual act.

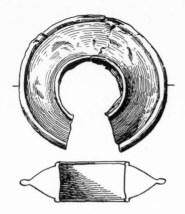

Fig. 46 Highdown Hill, Sussex. Gold ring. Diam. 1.5 ins

Two stories of the discovery of Late Bronze Age gold ornaments have passed into the annals of Sussex archaeology. In 1806 a one-eyed man called Jumper Hutches was beachcombing after a cliff fall at Beachy Head. He saw protruding from the cliff-face what was afterwards recognised as a bronze axe, and his subsequent search of the beach led him to find four penannular gold bracelets, three with expanded trumpet-shaped terminals. The axe was of the looped and winged variety and the other bronze saved was a small part of the hilt of a carp's-tongue sword. Both belong to a late phase of the late Bronze Age, probably to the seventh century B C. There are several accounts of the discovery which do not always agree in detail.

Plate 39

The Mountfield Treasure was ploughed up in 1863 on a farm near Battle. It seems to have consisted of a large torc or necklet with trumpet-shaped terminals and gold rings attached to it, bracelets, small rings and possibly ingots of raw gold. The finder sold the objects as old brass for 5s 6d; they were later sold for some £500 to a London dealer who melted them down. The Crown then put in a claim and the gold was held to be Treasure Trove; the men concerned in its disposal were held to be guilty of concealment and fined its full bullion value.

Further Sussex-coast discoveries include five gold armlets from the beach at Eastbourne and others from the beach at Selsey and

Fig. 46

from Cuckmere Haven. In 1901 a hollow penannular gold ring of triangular section, a broad-bladed chisel and a bronze tanged knife were recovered from a Saxon cemetery within the small Iron Age hill-fort on Highdown Hill near Worthing.

Of the forty or so gold ornaments from Kent none has been found in a satisfactory archaeological context. Possible exceptions are two hoards of eight and nine bracelets found in 1906 and 1907 respectively at Bexley 'buried in the sand beneath what had been the floors of ancient hut-dwellings'. Here there were bracelets with thickened, crescentic and coiled terminals which were perhaps units of value since they fall according to their weight into a series of multiples and fractions of a unit. Eleven gold ornaments have been found at various times in the neigh-bourhood of Aylesford, an important crossing of the Medway. Four armlets, one with cupped terminals, are said to have been in a box found in the river, and two torcs and an armlet, all deliberately broken, dredged from the river are almost certainly votive offerings. The finest piece is the heavy and magnificent

Plate 41

torc from Dover here illustrated, and another notable piece is a heavy ribbed coil from Chatham. A recent discovery of two

Plate 40

bracelets in a now dry chalk valley at Walderslade, east of the Medway, and Mr M. S. Gordon's recognition of the two brace-lets in the Ashmolean as part of a hoard of three from Little Chart on the Great Stour do not detract in any way from the widespread pattern of coastal and riverine distribution.

The nature of the Irish and perhaps Welsh gold trade towards the south-east and so with Central Europe still remains to be studied locally but the great majority of its relics are certainly, on the basis of their typology, to be placed late in the Bronze Age.

At the end of the conventional Bronze Age with its settled farming economy and much increased availability of bronze tools and weapons the south-east of England, in common with some other regions, had begun to feel the influence of the Hallstatt culture of the Continental Iron Age.

CHAPTER VII

The Celtic Peoples

THE GEOGRAPHY of south-east England still continued to be a major influence in its later prehistory. The long coast line and the wide approach to the Thames directly in face of the Continent was open to both local intrusion and larger-scale invasion. Inland certain regions, among them the chalk Downs, provided a suitable background for the continuation and persistence of some native and local ways of life. The use of iron and a knowledge of iron-working was brought to the south-east by peoples from northern France and the Low Countries and their adventurous and refugee waves of immigration varied in direction and intensity in accordance with the degree of social and political pressure existing from time to time in their Continental homelands. The Iron Age is conventionally distinguished by three main cultural groups. The first, between the sixth and fourth centuries B C, brought equipment and pottery of a developed late Hallstatt type and the culture known here as Iron Age A. It was in essence a culture based on simple farming life. The second, the B groups, brought a well developed La Tène I continental culture notable for its fine pottery and metalwork, and their settlements of small bands led by chieftains and warriors were extensive in the third and second centuries B C. In the south-east they sometimes replaced, sometimes mingled with, and sometimes kept apart from the earlier arrivals and the native inhabitants. The third immigration, that of the C groups, started to arrive late in the second century B C largely as a result of the Germanic, and later Roman, invasions of Gaul. In the south-east of England groups and tribes of the Belgae who had already entered into the Continental La Tène III phase of culture were its constituents, and Iron Age C lasted until the middle years of the first century B C or, more strictly perhaps, until A D 43. In another way chronology is sometimes set out in three periods, namely Period I from say 550 to 350; Period II from 350 to 150; and Period III from 150 to the Roman Conquest.

This is of course a very broad and greatly simplified outline based chiefly on Professor Hawkes' now classic 'ABC of the British Iron Age'. His scheme embracing the Southern Pro-vince, namely the regions of East Kent/Medway, Thames/Wealden and the South Downs, published in 1961 as part of a major study, provides full details and documentation for a thorough consideration of this very complex problem. In Sussex alone the Iron Age groups and phases, partly cultural and partly chronological, have been recognised as A1, A2, B, AB, a complex Wealden Culture derived from A and including 'Marnian' traits which in turn was to influence a South-eastern B culture from a source in north-west France, C1, C2, and even ABC. In a special study of the pottery Messrs Wilson and Burstow emphasised strong local differences from the normal general types. These differences were there from the beginning, and only some of the incoming types of pottery left their marks in the later styles.

In Surrey also there is a great complexity due to some extent, as Dr Gordon Copley has pointed out, to the intensive research undertaken by local archaeologists. For such work there can be nothing but praise, but the time has now come for a fresh approach. There are welcome signs that it is on the way.

For example, Dr F. R. Hodson has studied again a well-known group of pottery found many years ago at Eastbourne, Sussex, and hitherto regarded as including evidence of Hallstatt culture, and he has also raised doubts about the nature of 'Marnian' influence and in wider terms about the whole system of classifying the British Iron Age. This he followed by a new view of cultural grouping, bearing in mind that there are still major gaps in the evidence available. In summary Dr Hodson puts forward three major cultural divisions: (1) The Arras Culture, an early La

Tène group based on East Yorkshire which does not concern the south-east, (2) The Aylesford Culture, a late La Tène group centred on Kent, Essex and Hertfordshire, and (3) a series of regional groups, to be known as the Woodbury Culture after the well-known Wessex Iron Age farmstead, which are related by major cultural features and traditions, among them round-plan houses, bone or antler weaving-combs and ring-headed pins of iron with a characteristically bent shaft. All are traditions surviving from our native Bronze Age. In this light further studies of metal and pottery styles and of the construction of defended enclosures and hill-forts are clearly desirable, and much will depend on the detailed stratigraphical and statistical reports of future excavators. In the past in south-east England the many sites have yielded all too few relics, often as acci-dental discoveries and sometimes by excavation in the fashion used a generation ago. Meanwhile it should be emphasised that some sites exhibit a pattern of settlement little different from that of the local Late Bronze Age. Features of corn-growing and storage link Iron Age with Bronze Age traditions as does the system of settled cultivation associated with square fields of the familiar 'Celtic' pattern.

The Aylesford Culture is part of the history of British antiquity. Some eighty years ago the sharp eyes of a boy saw pieces of mouldering bronze in the old sand-pit at Aylesford, Kent, and Sir Arthur Evans, on a chance visit to collect flint implements, was thus led to the excavation of an 'ancient British' urn-field. His recognition of its Gaulish and Belgic character and 'Old Venetian (Illyro-Italic)' source opened a new chapter in the history of ancient Britain, a chapter which was further extended after the excavation in 1925 of another Late Celtic urn-field at Swarling near Canterbury. This chapter has now been re-written by Dr Ann Birchall in a brilliant study of the Aylesford-Swarling Culture and its continental analogues. Her suggestion of a restriction in date to a period of about 50–30 BC to 10 BC is indeed a novel one, and it contrasts with the evidence of a strong wave of Gallo-Belgic C coinage in the south-east about 100 BC. More recently still Professor Hawkes has had some new thoughts on the Belgae which suggest that the evidence of texts and coins need not 'drown' that from archaeology. What is needed, he says, is more planned excavation and with this no one will disagree.

These, then, are some of the problems which must be faced at this moment in any synthesis of cultural groupings and chronology in the pre-Roman Iron Age of south-east England. It is not a task which can be undertaken within the set limits of this book; the most that can be attempted here is a wide outline survey and the provision of a fairly detailed bibliography.

FARMSTEADS AND OPEN SETTLEMENTS

There is evidence of almost one hundred Iron Age farmsteads and open settlements in south-east England. That most of these are in Sussex is a reflection of the early interest and field-work of the archaeologists of that county but nowhere has there yet been excavated a site of the size and archaeological background of Little Woodbury, Wiltshire, with its circular houses, store-pits, granaries, drying-racks, hand-made pottery, and evidence of spinning, weaving and the rearing and ranching of cattle, sheep, goats and swine. Such sites as there are, however, must be set against this same sort of early Iron Age A background. It appears in its simplest form in the huts terraced into the steep North Downs at Harting Hill, Sussex, with their entrance slabs flanked by doorposts, primitive roof-supports, hearths and post-holes for looms, and no more than a few sherds of Iron Age A pottery. Pottery of much the same kind was used by early immigrants who made landfall on the coast of Thanet and in the neighbourhood of Deal and Walmer in East Kent. Intermediate progress westward along the North Downs Trackway is marked by a settlement on the valley brick-earth at

Canterbury and by a number of settlements on the loam- and sand-covered dip-slopes of the North Downs. The farmers of Iron Age A, some of whom had already been influenced by the peoples of the Marne, also entered the south-east by way of the Thames as is indicated by their settlements at Crayford, Kingston and Esher, between Croydon and Leatherhead, in the Guildford-Farnham region, and by the large number of tools and weapons dredged from the river itself.

It is to the Sussex hamlets, be they agricultural or pastoral, that we must turn for evidence of daily life. Close to the well-known Bronze Age site at Park Brow, Sompting, mentioned in the previous chapter, were excavated in 1924 the post-holes of two timber structures and several presumably covered storage pits; the inhabitants of the settlement no doubt worked in the 'Celtic' fields, some of which may still be seen near by. The most interesting discovery was a silver finger-ring of Swiss Early La Tène form (perhaps 325–250 BC); there was also an iron ring-headed pin. Spinning and weaving are attested by spindle-whorls, triangular loom-weights of clay and a bone weaving-comb, while saddle querns and carbonised grain point to agriculture and the bones of pigs, oxen, sheep and horses to a pastoral life. This settlement seems to have flourished between 400 and, say, 250 BC. By the first century BC it had been aban-doned in favour of a site farther down the southern slope of the hill (Park Brow II, which at one time was regarded as a 'Marnian' settlement), but its inhabitants continued to use the same fields and farming went on in much the same way well into Roman times, indeed until the end of the third century AD when the farmsteads were destroyed by fire. A similar farmstead existed at Findon Park on the Downs west of Park Brow. Eleven of its granary-pits were excavated many years ago. The method of storage has been studied by Mr J. R. B. Arthur in a consideration of a pit found in 1951 at Wickbourne, Littlehampton, where carbonised spelt was found to be heat-dried and covered by layers of a previously heated red-oxide clay. Mr Arthur also explains why this carbonised grain would not grow to-day if such an experiment were attempted.

Fig. 44

The downland patchwork of 'Celtic' field-systems is well illustrated at Old Kiln Bottom, Lullington, where farmsteads of the Late Bronze Age and Early Iron Age underlie later fields and their roadways.

Another Sussex site of interest, Muntham Court, Findon, excavated by Mr G. H. Holleyman, revealed a maze of more than 900 post-holes, depressions and bedding-trenches around and under a circular Romano-British shrine. The compound was enclosed by a palisade. No huts or hearths were found, but clay loom-weights, spindle-whorls, quantities of animal bones and a fair range of 'Sussex Iron Age A' pottery indicate the nature of the settlement.

The excavation of a Woodbury type of farmstead at Hawks Hill, Leatherhead, Surrey, in 1961–3 disclosed twelve storage pits and the post-holes of hay drying-racks and two granary platforms. There were seven main classes of pottery of wide affinities which suggested occupation over a long period beginning early in Iron Age A. Bones of cattle, sheep, pig and horse point to a highly developed animal husbandry which may have included ritual slaughter and pit-storage, and possibly a hide-burial. The report includes a summary account of the Iron Age in Surrey. It seems likely that the circular ditched settlement at Carshalton, Surrey, excavated by Mr A. W. G. Lowther in 1946—an excavation much limited by the hospital buildings on the site—was essentially of a similar kind.

Plate 43

One of the most interesting Iron Age A settlements is that on the valley brick-earth at Canterbury. Traces of it recovered by excavation include a ditch to which was later added a massive timber palisade. Pottery from the bottom of the ditch was rough and poorly made and was not, it is thought, earlier than 250–200 BC in date. According to one view, the palisade is best explained as a defence against invaders from the Marne. The site was abandoned at a date unknown, the palisade decayed and the whole area was sealed by later deposits which were not disturbed until the coming of the Belgae.

Farming was also practised on a fairly extended scale by the peoples of Sussex in Iron Age C. The interior of the hill-fort at Cissbury was put under plough, Park Brow and Kingston Buci continued, and new farmsteads were laid out particularly in the region between the Adur and Ouse, notably above the hill-fort on Thundersbarrow Hill where the magnificent roadway still to be seen may belong to this time, and outside the hill-fort at the Dyke. Many continued to flourish in the Roman period. In Kent, at Sturry and near Fordwich down-stream from Canterbury, Mr Frank Jenkins has recently examined two farmsteads of the later Belgic period both bounded by fenced-ditch enclosures for the retention of livestock and one with a timber-framed wattle-and-daub hut. The pottery on both sites can be dated between A D 10 and 43, and pottery of the same kind, perhaps thrown out as domestic and byre 'muck', is often found in quantities on the surface of the fields in the district.

In Belgic times, so far as is at present known, there were three major open settlements or oppida in the south-east. At Canterbury the open settlement, its site determined by a convenient river-crossing, a branch of the North Downs Trackway and good agricultural loam in the valley-bottoms, lay on both banks of the Stour. It was a widely scattered settlement of circular or sub-rectangular timber huts provided with drainage gullies and sometimes with hearths of crudely baked clay, the first tiles to be made in Britain. The superimposed gravel or clay floors were filled with household rubbish and occasionally the huts were provided with small ovens outside. Oyster and mussel shells, bones of oxen, sheep and pigs and the sawn tines of antlers give a good indication of the variety of food available. The number of much earlier barbaric speculum coins found in Canterbury

Plate 42

suggests a contact with pre-Belgic native peoples, but there is no certainty for this money was in use at least until the mid first-century A D. An important discovery was a unique silver coin of VODENOS the Belgic ruler who followed Dubnovellaunus and whose kingdom seems to have been confined to the east of the Medway. On the east bank of the Medway another oppidum of some size which apparently possessed its own mint was to be followed by the Roman town of Rochester; traces of a settlement have been found, and the oppidum may perhaps lie below the foundations of the existing Norman castle. A branch of the North Downs Trackway runs near by, and the Medway was easily fordable.

At Selsey Bill on the coast of Sussex the discovery at various times of more than 265 Celtic coins suggests the existence of an oppidum and a mint long since drowned by the encroachment of the sea. Such a settlement might well have had the Chichester Dykes system of earthworks as its northern protection and boundary not long before the Roman conquest.

HILL-FORTS

As the country became more widely populated with groups of newcomers from overseas added to the existing inhabitants it was inevitable that some sort of tribal organisation should come into being. In times of inter-tribal quarrels in the limited land available, the small open settlements and farmsteads provided insufficient shelter for man and beast and their place was taken by earthwork hill-forts. At first the hill-forts were perhaps the living-places of tribal chieftains and more certainly refuges for the tribe and its cattle at times of local quarrels and skirmishes; but later, and especially as a protection against warrior bands from the Continent, some of these hill-top enclosures were inhabited on a more permanent basis.

In the south-east as well as elsewhere in Britain the hill-forts and hill-top enclosures of the Iron Age are among the most spectacular of field antiquities. There are some fifty examples which range in size from the 1½ acres of the original enclosure on Thundersbarrow Hill, Sussex, to the 123 acres of Oldbury, Kent. They were situated to take full advantage of natural features and no doubt of the contemporary ecology. In Surrey the fort on St Anne's Hill, Chertsey, fronts the Thames and only a few miles to the south-east that on St George's Hill, Weybridge, controls both the Wey and the Mole, a short distance from their outfalls into the Thames. The Caburn, the Trundle, Cissbury and Torberry were each central refuges in blocks of Sussex downland delimited by rivers, indeed the Adur may have marked a political or cultural division between the eastern and western downlands from the third century BC, so generally different are the two groups of hill-forts in their characteristic features. The situation of Oldbury at the natural northern gateway to the Weald reflects a remarkable sense of both strategy and tactics.

In general the earliest hill-forts consist of a single ditch and protecting rampart with simple entrances, though such enclosures were still being built in the first century AD. Later forts were given timber-strengthened ramparts, more than one ditch and elabor-ately defended entrances, and there is often evidence of more than one period of construction and of subsequent modification. In a few instances there are fortuitous associations with earlier prehistory. The Trundle in Sussex encloses a Neolithic cause-wayed enclosure, the forts of Cissbury and Harrow Hill cut through or overlie Neolithic-Bronze Age flint-mines; the unusual triangular-shaped fort on Seaford Cliffs seems on the other hand to have been built with deference to a barrow of probable Bronze Age date.

Plate 45
Plate 11

The origins, variety and cultural significance of the south-eastern hill-forts are here best considered in an account of several outstanding examples, beginning with those of the Sussex Downlands, many of which were excavated some years ago.

The prominent downland hill of Mount Caburn near Lewes was inhabited perhaps as early as the sixth century B C by simple farming peoples using a Hallstatt type of pottery. They were part of a large group widely spread in the coastal regions between East Anglia and Dorset, and their maritime rather than Wessex contacts seem assured. It was not until their existence was threatened by the expansion of iron-workers from West Sussex towards the Weald and eastward along the Downs that a simple defensive enclosure of $3\frac{1}{2}$ acres was built. The slight bank and ditch suggest hasty measures. The life of the peaceful agricul-turists continued, as is shown by a large number of granary-pits—about 140 of these pits in which parched corn was stored before being ground in revolving handmills were excavated—by the remains of wattle huts with daub walls and doors with iron latches, by spindle-whorls of clay or stone, loom-weights of chalk, bone weaving-combs, iron sickles, bill-hooks and plough-shares. More personal objects include an iron razor and safety-pins, bronze brooches and a finger-ring and bone and bronze dress-fasteners. A blue glass bead, a lead weight and nine tin or speculum coins, the earliest native coins in Britain, show something of trading connections. Bones of horses, cattle, sheep, pigs and red deer and the calcified faeces of dogs point to pastoral and hunting activities. There is little evidence of pottery-making, though the characteristic Wealden pottery of the iron-workers was used in some quantity and suggests that the hill-fort was an established centre of descendants of the old 'South-Eastern Second B' cultural group.

The conservative native inhabitants of Mount Caburn con-tinued their peaceful life until the threat of Belgic penetration or of Roman attack obliged them to re-fortify the hill-top by con-structing a massive outer rampart faced and strengthened with timber and a very wide flat-bottomed ditch. To the present day the rampart still stands twenty feet above the bottom of the distinctive ditch, a reminder that such were the defensive measures used by the Gauls against Julius Caesar nearly a century before Roman troops fired the timber gateway of Mount Caburn and left there the trappings and scabbards of their swords.

Cissbury, high on a chalk spur between the Adur and the Arun, is generally recognised as the second most famous of the Sussex downland hill-forts. Its oval outline encloses 60 acres and its banks and ditch together occupy a further 18 acres. The hill-top had been occupied by people using a Hallstatt type of pottery but the defences, which enclosed a group of Neolithic-Bronze Age flint mines, were not raised before about 250 BC. Of particular interest is the 30 foot-wide chalk rampart revetted with timber on its outer face, thus providing a rampart-walk, and held rigid within by timber cross-beams. It has been calculated that the revetment required from 8,000 to 10,000 tree trunks of about nine inches in diameter and at least fifteen feet in length. Within two centuries this great earthwork had decayed and collapsed and in Roman times the interior came under cultivation, as is clear from the outline banks of the squarish Celtic-type fields. Towards the end of the Roman period the deserted site was re-fortified, principally by the addition of a turf wall on the top of the rampart, perhaps as a defence against Saxon raiders. To this time belong late Roman rubbish pits dug into the cultivation lynchets and the sites of the rectangular huts still to be seen in favourable conditions.

CISSBURY

Plate 11

Fig. 47

The Iron Age hill-fort surrounding the Neolithic causewayed enclosure at The Trundle on the chalk downs of West Sussex is octagonal in plan and its twelve-and-a-half acres are enclosed by a rampart, outer ditch and a counterscarp bank. Its two entrances, defended by slingers' platforms, are in-turned for additional protection and excavation of the east gate has shown, on the evidence of its post-holes, three successive stages of timber gate-ways and, in the second stage, of a timber revetment along

THE

TRUNDLE

Plate 45

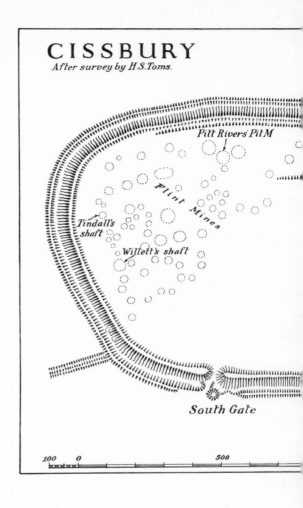

CISSBURY
After survey by H.S.Toms.

Pitt Rivers'Pit M

Flint Mines

Tindall's shaft

Willett's shaft

South Gate

100   0   500

Fig. 47   Cissbury Camp, Sussex

the walls of the entrance. The last phase, begun about 50 BC, which was to include a massive double gate had not been completed when the fort was abandoned. Altogether the site seems to have been occupied for some two centuries, and in conventional terms it would be ascribed to Iron Age B of West Sussex.

148

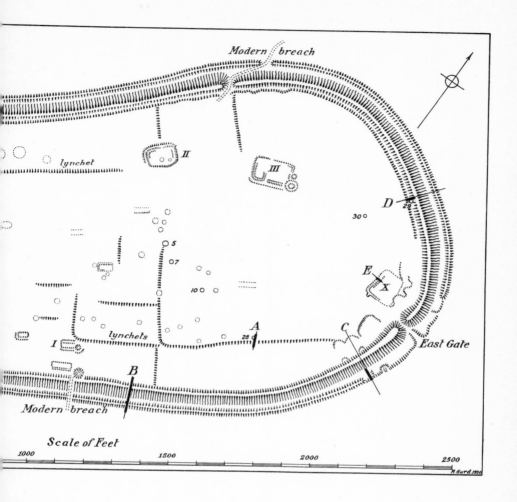

The downs at Hollingbury, north of Brighton, were defended by a simple rectangular earthwork of bank and ditch as early as the fifth century B C. The main features to be seen at the present time are part of an enlargement of the original fort made about 250 B C, but these features give but little idea of the appearance of the massive original earthworks which enclosed some nine acres of the hill top. In plan the fort was almost square, with two entrances, and its six-foot-high rampart of chalk rubble was faced on the exterior and laced in the interior with massive timber beams and logs. A deep flat-bottomed ditch and a flat berm ten feet wide between ditch and rampart added to the strength of the site which had an obvious military purpose. The plan of the east gate recovered by excavation showed the post-holes of one large single gateway; the west gate, which has not been excavated, has an in-turned entrance.

DEVIL'S
DYKE
Plate I

On the landward escarpment of the South Downs some four miles north-west of Hollingbury is the Devil's Dyke, an example of a fort with substantial ramparts across the neck of a promontory which needed much less artificial defence on its steep natural slopes. A limited excavation suggested its intermittent use between 500–250 BC. A later farming settlement outside the fort proper was associated with coins of Epaticcus and the Emperor Claudius, but one farm hut at least stood inside.

HASCOMBE
HILL

Hascombe Hill, a promontory fort on the Greensand ridge of Surrey, has a single ditch and rampart across a narrow neck of land, with one simple entrance, and the natural steep slope of the hill made any further defence, apart from a ditch below the brow of the hill, unnecessary. Pottery and other material excavated here in 1931 suggest a date late in the first century BC.

ANSTIEBURY,
HOLMBURY,
HAMMER
WOOD,
DRY HILL

Several hill-forts on the Greensand ridges may well mark the eastern and northern expansion of the West Sussex Wealden peoples in their search for iron ore. Anstiebury and Holmbury, excavated in 1930, Hammer Wood, Iping, a promontory fort discovered in 1956 from an air-photograph and excavated in 1957, and Dry Hill, Lingfield, were occupied by these Wealden folk whose culture reflected continental Hallstatt, La Tène and native features: Holmbury seems to have been built only shortly

Fig. 48   Oldbury Camp, Ightham, Kent

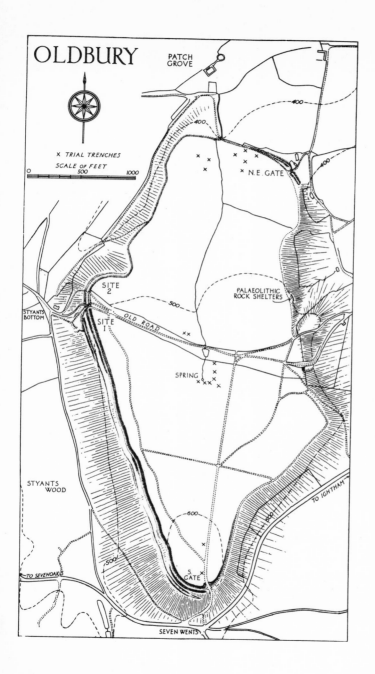

OLDBURY

PATCH GROVE

✕ TRIAL TRENCHES

SCALE OF FEET
0   500   1000

400

400

400

N.E. GATE

SITE 2

STYANTS BOTTOM

SITE 1

OLD ROAD

500

PALAEOLITHIC ROCK SHELTERS

SPRING

STYANTS WOOD

600

TO IGHTHAM

500

TO SEVENOAKS

500

S. GATE

SEVEN WENTS

before the Roman Conquest. Two of the Wealden hill-forts are of especial interest.

Oldbury in Kent, excavated in 1938, lies on a Greensand hill which has a considerable natural strength of defence, commands a natural corridor from the north into the Weald, and so an important crossing of the Medway at Tonbridge. The hill-fort, with its gateways at the north and south, was deliberately placed to control this route. In the first part of its life, about 100 BC, the fort consisted of a small rampart, a five-foot-deep V-shaped ditch, and gateways of simple form. Its builders, men of the Wealden group, evidently worked on a basis of common sense rather than upon any preconceived theory of construction. No traces of interior structures or of more than a sporadic occupation were found. In the second major period of its life the ramparts of the fort were built up and strengthened, the ditch widened and given a broad flat bottom, and the gateways remodelled with

Plate 46

elaborate in-turned entrances. Many sling stones found on the outer slopes of the ramparts and evidence of the burning of the north gate suggests that the fort had been stormed by the enemy against whom its defences had been strengthened. The characteristic wide-bottomed ditch, as at the Caburn, points perhaps to the identification of the enemy with the advancing troops of Claudius. It has been suggested, however, that the latest re-fortification of both Mount Caburn and Oldbury may reflect a resistance to expansion in the time of Catuvellaunus, the inter-tribal differences between the Catuvellauni and the Atrebates when Kent was invaded by Eppillus, or a defence against the westward movement of the Belgae.

The large hill-fort at Holwood Park, Keston, Kent, excavated between 1956 and 60 has in places three lines of closely set banks and ditches, and a slighter earthwork near by may be a cattle-compound associated with the fort. Both appear to date in the second century BC. Not far away, on the Lower Greensand, stands the promontory hill-fort of Squerryes Park, Westerham, which excavations in 1961–2 suggest belongs to the first century BC, though the evidence is not as clear as could be wished. Also on the Greensand, south of Maidstone, is a hill-fort at Boughton Quarry which has features in common with the hill-forts of northern France.

The most recently excavated hill-fort is High Rocks, Tunbridge Wells, upon which Mr James Money will shortly publish a full report and reconsider certain aspects of the Iron Age in south-east England. It is sited with due regard to the precipitous rocks of the northern Greensand ridge and covers some 20 acres. The first fort, built about 100 BC, had a single rampart and simple ditch cut into the natural rock. At some time in the middle of the first century BC further ramparts faced or crested with stone were built inside the earlier structure (the expansion was controlled by the natural lie of the land), an in-turned eastern entrance with elaborate outworks constructed, and a flat-bottomed ditch dug as at Oldbury and the Caburn.

HIGH ROCKS

The hill-fort at Bigbury (Bigberry) some two miles west of Canterbury is generally thought to be the site of the strongly fortified native *oppidum* which Caesar describes as being already prepared for inter-tribal warfare when it was stormed by the Seventh legion during his second invasion. The main defences, a wide ditch with an inner bank and a counterscarp bank, follow generally the 200-foot contour and the polygonal plan encloses some 25 acres; on the north side is a crescent-shaped enclosure of a further eight acres, which was probably a cattle-compound. A branch of the North Downs Trackway passes through the hill-fort from east to west, its entrance at the east defended by two deep ditches and an outer bank, the gaps through which were made in zigzag fashion for greater protection.

BIGBURY

Fig. 49

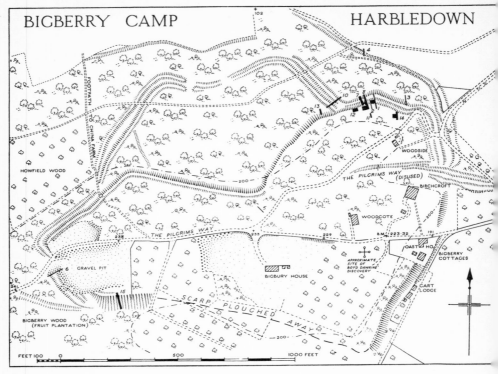

BIGBERRY CAMP   102   HARBLEDOWN

Fig. 49   Bigbury (Bigberry) Camp, Harbledown, Kent

Plates 47–50   Many casual discoveries made in the course of gravel-digging
at Bigbury during the nineteenth century throw considerable
light on its day-to-day life without providing a precise chronology.
Few weapons are known, but iron agricultural tools, axes, adzes,
hammers, chisels, plough coulters, sickles and bill-hooks, are
common. There is also kitchen equipment, iron pot-hooks,
hangers for cauldrons and the tripods from which they were
hung, the latter of a type which Professor Stuart Piggott notes
in a 'Common Market area from Britain to Czechoslovakia
and Austria'. A scrap of an iron tyre, linch-pins with bronze
mounts, three-link snaffle-bits of Yorkshire type and harness

154

fittings represent the equipment of a well-to-do farming community rather than a military force. A single low-standing fire-dog, now badly corroded but of fine design and skilful workmanship, iron gang-chains with barrel locks and a series of fetters, a reminder of the slave-trade between Britain and Gaul, and of the probability that the Bigbury farmers themselves used slave labour, are among some of the most interesting discoveries made.

Excavations in 1933–4 yielded pottery from the primary silt of the main ditch and the contemporary occupation layers. The rough hand-made pottery of gritted fabric may belong to a pre-Belgic occupation as may some of the metalwork, but several wheel-turned pots of good quality fabric are certainly products of the Aylesford-Swarling peoples. More recent excavations in the inner ditch near the east entrance by Mr Frank Jenkins revealed a causeway; pottery from the primary silt was of Iron Age A character, a clay sling-bolt was found in the same deposit, and there was evidence of a palisade in the bottom of the ditch. Clearly a hill-fort existed here before the time of the Belgae. The chronological problems of this interesting and important site are also indicated by the discovery of two fine pieces of early second-century A D glassware.

METALWORKING

Apart from the Forest of Dean, the Weald was the principal centre of iron-mining in Britain. Small domestic bloomeries were used almost throughout the conventional Iron Age but it was not until the middle of the first century B C that the industry was established on a commercial scale. To begin with the poorer quality of ironstones, especially carstone from exposures of the Folkestone Beds within easy reach of the Sussex downland settlements, provided raw material for bloomeries which were probably nomadic. Only later, after peoples of the Wealden Culture had explored the forests of the Weald and reached its

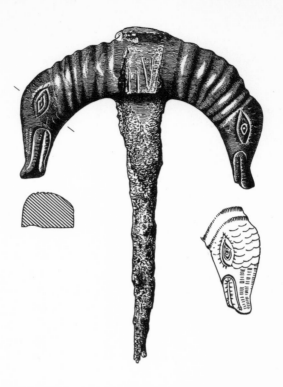

Fig. 50   Hassocks, Sussex. Bronze-mounted linch-pin. Length 5.7 ins

northern border, was the much richer ironstone from the Wadhurst Clay and Ashdown Sand worked on sites which readily
provided running water and the timber necessary for charcoal
fuel. Settlements of ironworkers have been found at Crowhurst,
Ticehurst and Dallington; those at Saxonbury on the central
Wealden Ridge and at West Hoathly were defended, possibly
against Belgic pressure from beyond the Medway, though some
of the bloomeries must have supplied the raw material used in
quantity by the Belgae themselves. The history of the iron
industry of the Weald in all its aspects is now being studied anew
by the Wealden Iron Research Group, and as a result we shall

Fig. 51   Bapchild, Kent. Enamelled bronze terret. Diam. 3.2 ins

certainly know more about such matters as the production of
domestic and agricultural tools and appliances, of weapons and
of the horse-gear and slave-gang chains exemplified, for instance,
at Bigbury. We may also learn something about the standing and
organisation of the ironsmiths who were perhaps a privileged
class: who, for example, commissioned and who made the
bronze-headed Celtic linch-pin found in a Roman rubbish pit
at Hassocks, Sussex?

Fig. 50

Little is known about the Iron Age metal workshops, but a
good deal about one of their products, the daggers which include
some of the earliest ironwork made in Britain. These very personal
tools and weapons of many uses are restricted, as Professor E. M.
Jope has shown, to an area of the Lower and Middle Thames
and all have been dredged from the bed of the river. Many are
complete with their sheaths, which may suggest that they were
votive offerings, and nearly all are distinguished by a high-grade
workmanship which could only have been sponsored by an
aristocratic element among the early peasants and farmers. In
date they cover a period from the sixth century to the latter
fourth-century B C; they were not imports and in design and
execution their workmanship reflects traditions continued from
the Late Bronze Age.

Plates 51–53

Plate 58
Plate 57

Fig. 51

Outstanding among metal prestige objects are the splendid bronze shield of insular late La Tène style from the Thames at Battersea, surely a votive offering, and the bronze helmet with studs once covered with red enamel from the Thames at Waterloo Bridge, probably an accidental loss in the first century B C. One of the finest pieces of small enamel work from the south-east is a bronze terret from Bapchild, Kent, with a ground of crimson and a meander pattern ornamented with spots of cobalt blue.

BURIALS

Fig. 52

Plate 54

Plate 55

There is little evidence of burial customs in the earlier phases of the Iron Age. A cremation in an urn of Hallstatt type at Park Brow, Sompting, an inhumation with a perhaps early imitation Belgic butt-beaker at Eastbourne, and a single cremation at the Caburn are all that can be reliably quoted. It is otherwise with the flat-grave cremation burials of the Belgae at the type-sites of Aylesford, Swarling and Deal. Carefully made graves, some lined with flints or chalk and the contents protected by stones, and a disposition in 'family circles' which must surely have been marked in some way on the surface, denote a strong feeling for ritual. The wealth of the contents, fine distinctive pottery, bronze vessels, bronze brooches, buckets and a tankard of wood with bronze mounts and enamel studs on the handle indicate the burials of an aristocracy. At Aylesford a bronze patella and a bronze oenochoe, vessels with a ritual significance, and bronze brooches both there and at Swarling can be compared with similar types from the Ornavasso cemetery in northern Italy. The human mask on the handle-mounting of the Aylesford bucket has been described as the grandest of the minor pieces of Celtic metalwork in Britain, a 'surrealist' vision, and the pattern of the horse-like creatures on its rim is indeed a remarkable statement of abstract masses. The bronze mount of a bucket from Boughton Aluph in the Stour valley is another notable example of this highly stylized artistic convention, here representing a horned god.

Fig. 52 Aylesford Cemetery, Kent. Grave as recorded in 1890

On the evidence now available Dr Ann Birchall has done much to reconstitute the grave-groups, but there was more found at Aylesford than Evans or the London collectors ever knew.

Several shrines and temples with Romano-Celtic associations are noted in the following chapter. Shrines which can be more properly, though not absolutely certainly, attributed to the pre-Roman Iron Age are Blue Bell Hill, Aylesford, on the escarp-ment of the North Downs above the site of the Belgic urn-field, and Worth, a coastal site in East Kent. Next to nothing is known about Blue Bell Hill. Worth, dug up in 1925, yielded fragments of a bronze statuette of Mars or Minerva and these as well as a Romano⁄Celtic plan indicate a Roman use, but a bone weaving⁄comb and a very mixed collection of Iron Age pottery point to a much earlier occupation over a long period as might be expected in this region of Kent. A spread of Iron Age coins close to the Romano⁄Celtic temple of Farley Heath, Surrey, also suggests a continuity of use. Mention should also be made of the shafts and deep pits—not dene⁄holes—described in the older archaeological literature: some may well have a ritual significance to be asso⁄ciated with the Iron Age. The shaft at Keston, Kent, 16 feet deep and 11 feet in diameter, which contained the cremations of two dogs and fragments of indeterminate pottery at its base may perhaps be set against a Celtic background though the ritual sense of the dogs is a Romano⁄Gaulish feature.

COINAGE

The many discoveries of Belgic coins, inscribed and uninscribed, of gold, silver and tin, singly and in hoards, have long been a notable feature of south⁄eastern archaeology. Much has been said, and guessed, about the distribution of the inscribed series and of their possible significance in the interpretation of political events and development. A new and very detailed study by Mr D. F. Allen pays great attention to typology as well as to distribution and chronology. Six primary and secondary waves of invasion are recognised by Mr Allen as products of major folk⁄movements from Belgic Gaul and the coins do not at once indicate the direction and extent of trade. They are widely spread in Kent, Surrey and Sussex, usually in relation to sea, river and downland natural routes of communication. The earliest coins are of continental origin and it seems that later coins of a similar origin and the native issues to which they gave rise must all be regarded as the property of warrior bands. Only the Armorican

Plate 56

gold and silver coins which found their way to the coasts of
Kent and Sussex came by way of trade. For the rest, the coins
came into the south-east by a complex series of movements, first
by bands of warrior-adventurers and later by settlers who appear
to have supplanted the native peasants. The existence of mints at
Rochester and Selsey has already been noted. In Kent, the main
transit region, seven hoards are recorded, two in hollow flint
money-boxes and one of more than 600 coins many of which
were said to be in a wooden box. Six hoards, including one of
forgeries, are known from Sussex and one from Surrey. Five
winged iron bars were found in the hill-fort at Bigbury: they
are much more likely to be plough-shares than currency bars of
the generally accepted type.

At the time of the Conquest south-east England, always in close
touch with Gaul, had already acquired a considerable degree of
Romanisation. That it was set against a background of relatively
stable and certainly effective Belgic central government ensured
its continued progress. Caesar in two well-known passages
mentions Kent, the most civilised of all the regions in Britain,
over which four several kings reigned. On the evidence of coins
it was later ruled by Dubnovellaunus of the Trinovantes, the
first Kentish king to inscribe his coins, then by Eppillus, son of
Tincommius of the Atrebates, and then by Cunobelin, that
most famous prince of the Catuvellauni, son of Tasciovanus.
The province of Cunobelin, most of it north of the Thames, also
included the greater part of Kent and north-east Surrey; the area
controlled by the Atrebates, centred on Selsey and Silchester,
also included the western parts of Surrey and Sussex, while
between the two major tribal areas there still existed in east
Sussex, east Surrey and part of south-west Kent an enclave of the
old Wealden peoples who refused to conform with the Belgic
way of life.

CHAPTER VIII

The Roman Occupation

THE ARRIVAL of Caesar's expedition in 55 BC marks an outstanding point in the story of south-east Britain. Although from this time the assistance of historical record is intermittently available, and full and skilful use of it has been made by Professors Sheppard Frere and D. R. Dudley and Dr Graham Webster, history is not yet fully supported by archaeology. The reasons for the campaign against Britain, among them the probability of economic gain, an increase in personal prestige for its leader and the establishment of a secure frontier in face of Gaul, have often been set out, and do not call for discussion here.

The whole of the first campaign, a reconnaissance backed only by the slightest of direct intelligence, took place in less than a month. Moving down channel from the cliffs of Dover which were lined by British forces, Caesar beached his fleet near Deal leaving some of his transport vessels off-shore. A beach-head camp must have been established, though no trace of it has ever been located on this constantly changing coast-line and the fighting was, after the first struggle on the shore, in the nature of guerilla warfare. His boats damaged by storm, his transports unable to make the shore for the same reason, Caesar, after taking hostages and noting the possibilities of corn-production, returned to Gaul and the honour of a twenty-day *supplicatio* in Rome. The Ocean had been crossed.

The second expedition in 54 BC, much larger and much more carefully mounted, landed unopposed on the coast, presumably between Sandown and Walmer and a base-camp may have been built on the higher land near Worth though here again there is no archaeological evidence.

British forces gathered at a ford over the Stour, perhaps at Tonford, or, it may be, nearer the future site of Canterbury itself, were defeated after a day's severe fighting, and a camp of sufficient size to accommodate the large Roman force was built near by at a place which has not yet been located. The story of the storming of a newly-fortified native stronghold, the hill-fort at Bigbury above Tonford, by the Seventh Legion, shields held testudo-fashion above their heads, has passed into our national history. After a retreat to his base to repair storm-damaged transports, Caesar quickly moved westward aided by his strong force of cavalry and crossed the Thames at a difficult and the only available ford, possibly at Brentford Stakes but more probably lower down the river towards Southwark. His campaign on the northern side of the river in the home territory of Casivellaunus does not concern us here. Within two months he had made terms with the enemy, taken hostages, imposed a tribute and returned to Gaul.

The difficulties, and some of the certainties, of the political geography of Britain between the expeditions of Caesar and the invasion under Claudius have recently been studied in detail by Professor Frere and Mr A. L. F. Rivet. In common with Caesar's expeditions, the Claudian conquest had motives both political and personal. As a source of trade and revenue, for its mineral wealth, its production of corn ever necessary for the needs of the army, as well as for its man-power potential, Britain would form a desirable addition to the Empire, and, in the words of Professor Frere, 'world rule was part of the psychological inheritance of the Caesars.' Already the exiled Bericus, one of the sons of Cunobelin the greatest of the Belgic kings who controlled much of the south-east, had sought the aid of Rome, while his brothers Caratacus and Togodumnus who remained powerful in Britain expelled Verica of the Atrebates to Rome and themselves fomented trouble on the coast of Gaul as well as civil strife at home.

The invasion of Britain had been long awaited and its preparation was thorough. Four legions and auxiliaries set sail in

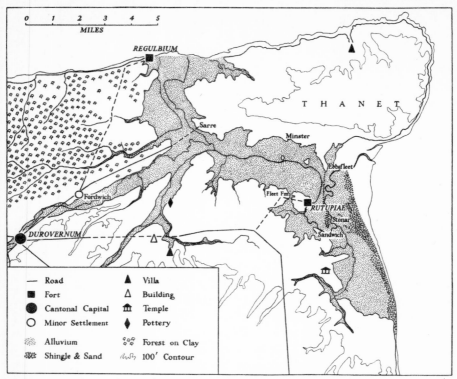

Fig. 53 North-east Kent in the Roman period

three divisions from Boulogne and landed unopposed, it seems on the balance of probabilities at Richborough. There were two engagements somewhere in East Kent with Caratacus and Togodumnus and then a decisive two-day battle at a crossing of the Medway at or near Rochester. The native troops retreated to the Thames at London where the Romans crossed the river by ford and bridge and so pursued their victorious course. Within three weeks the Claudian base in East Kent was firmly secure. Britain was part of the Empire, and the south-east was its official gateway. The slow process of full Romanisation had begun.

Throughout almost five centuries of Roman influence the peninsula of the south-east continued to be the main bridgehead for traffic between the Continental Empire and the island which became its Northern Province. Its road-system, beginning with *Fig. 53* a military and official highway linking the ports of disembarkation with the nodal crossing of the Thames at Londinium and thence eventually to the frontiers of the Province, was quickly supple-mented by roads serving the cantonal capitals of Durovernum Cantiacorum (Canterbury), Noviomagus Regnensium (Chi-chester), and the walled town at the crossing of the Medway, Durobrivae (Rochester). Other military requirements were met by roads from the four eastern forts of the Saxon Shore which converged on Canterbury. Over-all, a highly developed system provided ready oversea-transit, through-ways and local com-munication on a planned basis for the army, for administrators, for farmers and for traders.

The main military and official highway started at Rutupiae (Richborough), the earliest supply-base and for a time the chief *Fig. 54* port of Britain, going by way of Durovernum, Durobrivae and its bridge over the Medway, Vagniacae (Springhead), a posting-station with a group of temples, and Noviomagus (Crayford) at the crossing of the Darent, to Londinium. A settlement at Ospringe near Faversham may well represent a posting-station, the Durolevum of the Antonine Itinerary. The early use of the road is well attested by archaeological evidence, not least by a hoard of thirty-four aurei, some in almost mint-condition, found *Plate 59* just off its course at Bredgar in 1957; whether they were hidden by an army officer as part of his pay or by a native trader, these fine gold coins belong to the time of the Claudian invasion or very little later. The road continued in use during the Saxon period, when it probably received its name of Watling Street, and for long eras of history as the 'Dover Road' it was the principal link between London, Canterbury and the Channel

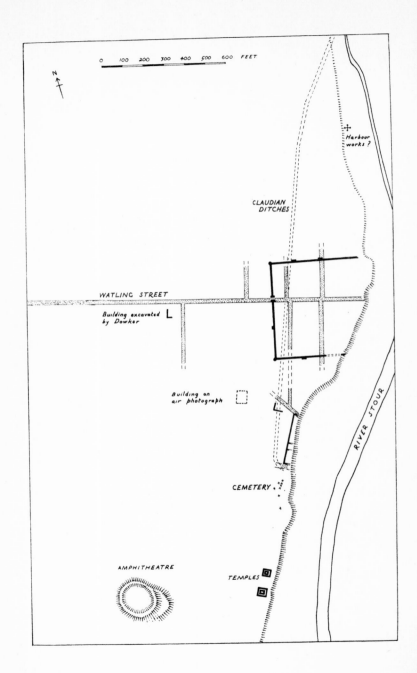

0   100   200   300   400   500   600   FEET

N

Harbour
works ?

CLAUDIAN
DITCHES

WATLING STREET

Building excavated
by Dowker

Building on
air photograph

RIVER STOUR

CEMETERY

AMPHITHEATRE

TEMPLES

crossing. The modern A2 highway follows much of the course of its Roman predecessor.

An important road ran southward from Rochester through the corn-growing lands of the Medway Valley to a large settlement at Maidstone in the ragstone country, to Benenden where there were traces of a paved ford at Iden Green, and so to the iron- and timber-producing region in the hinterland of a port at Hastings on the Channel coast. From Sutton Valence, on the ragstone hills a little south of Maidstone, there was a direct road to the Saxon Shore fort at Lympne and at Hempsted a branch road left in a north-eastward direction for Canterbury. Several sectors of these roads still remain to be traced on the ground; air-photographs continue to indicate missing and occasionally new alignments, and field archaeologists in Kent are now giving much attention to road chronology.

The early road system is equally evident in the western and central parts of south-east Britain. Stane Street, which led from Chichester north-eastward across the Downs through Pulborough, Billingshurst and Dorking to London, has been recognised as a Roman road since early times and has been studied in some detail. Two official posting-stations, both protected by rectangular earthwork enclosures, have been excavated. That at Hardham was in use between AD 50 and 150, when its place was perhaps taken by Pulborough; pre-Roman pottery suggests a connection with the native capital. Alfoldean, the second posting-station, with its stables, cart-sheds and simple lodgings flourished throughout the Roman occupation. A two-span bridge on stone piers, its foundations revealed by a drought in 1934, carried the road over the River Arun. The course of the road is still magnificently preserved on the crest of the Downs near Bignor Hill. Ewell, by the side of a natural spring on the line of the road in Surrey, seems by the range and variety of its antiquities to have grown into a pleasant residential settlement.

Fig. 54 Environs of Richborough, Kent

From Chichester, through a posting-station at Iping, a road ran north-westward with Calleva (Silchester) the cantonal capital of the Atrebates as its objective, and westward a major road travelled to Bitterne, the port of Clausentum, and so northward to Venta Belgarum of the Belgae (Winchester) with its road access to the Midlands, west country and frontier of Wales.

Two north-south secondary roads played an important part in the economic development of the central region. From Watling Street on the south-east side of London, a road which was already in use during the latter part of the first century ran by way of Edenbridge across the high ridges of Ashdown Forest to the neighbourhood of Lewes, with a westward link, part of the Sussex Greensand Way, to Hardham on Stane Street. It served no particular town or settlement but gave ready access to the depot of London for corn grown on the downland farms of East Sussex and the iron mined and timber felled in the central Weald. For many miles it is made up of iron-slag, and at Holtye near East Grinstead a length of the original surface with its wheel-ruts is preserved by the Sussex Archaeological Trust. It is said that the course of the road was revealed by a line of burnt corn when the buried iron-slag was struck by lightning. A roughly parallel road left Stane Street south-west of London, running by Selsfield Common, Ardingly and Burgess Hill to Hassocks (the site of a very large cemetery) where it was joined by the east-west road from Hardham and then continued in a short course to the Brighton Downs. Several minor trackways are related to it, and here again it is reasonable to suppose that the road linked the East Sussex cornlands with the market and collection centre in London. Many of the downland farm-tracks and field-ways and their terraced descents on the steep northern face of the Downs are still conspicuous features in the landscape.

There are two other roads for brief notice. From Chichester a road known as *stanstrete* in a land charter of A D 930 may earlier have served a populous Roman and pre-Roman settlement in

Plate 60

the plain of Selsey. From the Saxon Shore fort at Anderita (Pevensey) a road, its unusual curved route dictated by natural features, ran in a short westerly course towards the Ouse and the north/south trading routes already noted. The North Downs Trackway was still in local use in Roman times, but there is no evidence that it formed a through-route or that it was connected with the general road-system. It may have served, at least in its eastern sector, the invasion forces in A D 43, but such an association is no more than speculation.

Two suggested examples of the rectangular land division known as centuriation, one north of Rochester and the other near Ripe and Chalvington in Sussex, both associated with road-systems, are not fully accepted by all authorities.

A milestone found, it is said, at Shorne north of the Watling Street near Rochester, and another from Worthing in Sussex, well off the course of any known main road, do not add to our knowledge of the road system.

No one can discuss Roman roads in Britain without grateful acknowledgment to the extensive scholarly research of Mr Ivan D. Margary. A full account of the roads in the south-east, his own countryside, will be found in his books listed in the bibliography.

COMMUNICATIONS: WATER

Very little is known of the navigation of the Lower Thames and its Estuary, the all-important waterway which gave access to London throughout the Roman age. It cannot have been an easy passage. The large quantities of second-century Samian ware dredged from time to time from the Pudding Pan Rock, a shoal in the estuary off Whitstable, may well indicate the fate of one cargo vessel with an unhandy master in a north-east gale. A navigation mark on the fortlet at Hadleigh on the northern shore and another possibly at Shorne or Cliffe on the south bank may have assisted passage in the lower reaches. This fascinating problem, to which little attention has so far been paid, is greatly complicated by a considerable post-Roman depression in the surface of the land. Foundations of Roman huts, for example, were visible at low tide on the Essex foreshore some 40 years ago yet in Cliffe Marshes on the opposite Kentish bank traces of a timber jetty associated with the import of luxury second-century pottery were covered by a stratified deposit of silt 13 feet in depth.

The northern rivers, the Stour, Medway, Darent and Wey, and the Rother, Ouse, Adur, and Arun opening to the Channel, were in use from an early stage in the Roman period though once again next to nothing is known of their navigation. The small river Arun has the distinction of appearing under its Roman name of *Trisanto* in Ptolemy.

The Thames has yielded the remains of three known Roman boats. The first, uncovered near the east end of Westminster Bridge in 1910, was carvel-built of oak with an original length of some 60 feet and a beam of 16 feet; pulley-blocks, a belaying pin and coins of the latter part of the third century lay within it and a piece of the mast near by. Another boat of roughly the same dimensions and apparently dating in the late second century was noted in 1959 during building operations at Guy's Hospital, Southwark. The timbers, which were in a silted-up creek of the river, could not be fully excavated. And finally, in 1962, a carvel-built flat-bottom barge was excavated by the staff of the Guildhall Museum at Blackfriars Bridge. A worn coin of Domitian with Fortuna at the rudder of a ship on its reverse had been placed in the step of the mast, no doubt in the hope of securing fair winds. Most likely this boat with its cargo of ragstone from Kent sank by reason of its worm-ridden timbers.

MILITARY SITES

Within the enclave of survival of the old Wealden peoples there was resistance to the Belgae and perhaps to the forces under Claudius. The conservative inhabitants of the Caburn strongly re-fortified their hill-fort with massive new ramparts, a wide flat-bottomed ditch and a new gateway as did those who occupied the hill-fort at Oldbury in the northern part of the region. Their efforts were in vain. At Caburn the gateway was destroyed by fire; at Oldbury masses of slingstones were of no avail against the superior enemy forces.

Until recent years the only major archaeological evidence of the Claudian invasion under Aulus Plautius has been the bridge-head enclosure at Richborough marked by the excavated course of its parallel V-shaped ditches with a causeway and entrance. Such a camp, Dr Graham Webster points out, would accommodate tents for only 2,500 troops, far short of the legionary force assembled for the main invasion. Another camp may yet remain to be discovered. Richborough with its rows of timber-built granaries and warehouses quickly became the principal supply base in Britain and by AD 47 it was already providing for the needs of troops on the Trent-Severn frontier. The camp was sited on a tidal island, a natural harbour in the Wantsum Channel between Thanet and the mouth of the Stour. At its northern end this tidal channel was defended at Reculver by a small contemporary outpost fort covering but one acre and having a rampart-backed ditch crossed by a timber bridge. Pottery from the ditch-filling provides new and satisfactory evidence of its date. At Springhead on Watling Street part of a large first-century rectangular ditched enclosure surrounding the settlement has recently been discovered and this also is likely to be a Claudian work. Still further west at Fishbourne there is evidence of granaries or military store-buildings of Claudian date, possibly to house troops of the second legion under Vespasian, and in view of the organisation of the invasion, so well to be seen in Belgic Gaul, it would be surprising if other discoveries of the same sort do not remain to be made.

Of the nine British forts between the Wash and the Solent under the command of the Count of the Saxon Shore listed in

Fig. 55

Fig. 53

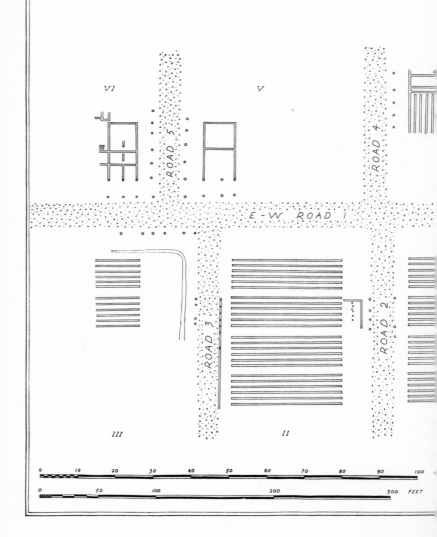

RICHBOROUGH CASTLE

THE CLAUDIAN SUPPLY BASE

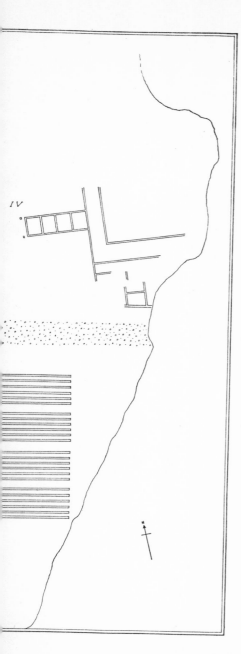

Fig. 55   Richborough, Kent. Lines of the timber buildings and roads of the Claudian supply base, as revealed by excavation

IV

the *Notitia Dignitatum*, five are sited on the south-east coast. They are Reculver *(Regulbium)*, Richborough *(Rutupiae)*, Dover *(Dubris)*, Lympne *(Lemanis)*, and Pevensey *(Anderita)*. All but Pevensey are at strategic points, all have good seaward communications and all, again except Pevensey, are well served by good roads. Defended anchorages and strong landward defence systems point to a mixed garrison of naval and military forces. Reculver and Richborough were on sites used in Claudian times; the fort at Reculver has features in common with standard Roman fortifications and with the East Anglian forts at Brancaster and Burgh Castle rather than with the thick tile-bonded walls and *ballista* towers of the others in the series. Reculver, as we shall see, was built in the early part of the third century and adapted in the latter part of the century at a time when the other members of the group were built in their characteristic style. It has usually been thought that these defences of 275–287 were against Saxon sea-raiders and later pirate-settlers, but there is now evidence that Carausius, the commander of the British Fleet who in 287 had usurped the title of Emperor in Britain and northern Gaul, built the forts and others on the Gaulish shore against possible official measures against him by Diocletian and Maximian. (A detailed account of the British Fleet is included by Professor Cunliffe in his Richborough Report noted below.)

RECULVER
Fig. 53
Plate 62

The northern part of the fort at Reculver has long since disappeared into the sea and during the gradual process of erosion the site yielded many relics of its antiquity though relatively few were ever recorded. Since 1952 the still existing features and others revealed by excavation have been studied by the Reculver Excavation Group, a highly organised team of amateur archaeologists directed by Mr Brian Philp assisted by Mr Harold Gough. This large square fort of some 8 acres, with rounded corners, was laid out with the standard grid pattern of roads, four gateways, an intervallum road at the foot of the internal ramp behind the wall which was itself defended by two steep outer ditches, a headquarters building, officers' quarters, barracks, stores and bath-houses. The record of a garrison of *Cohors I Baetasiorum* listed in the *Notitia* has been confirmed by the discovery of four bricks marked by the official stamp of the unit, and this unit may well have built the fort which on good archaeological evidence can now be dated early in the third century. Another very important discovery, parts of an inscription found in the ruined strong-room beneath the *sacellum* of the headquarters building, confirms the dating. It records the building of the *sacellum* and *basilica* by Fortunatus under a consular governor Aulus Triarius Rufinus: an official of this name was *consul ordinarius* in Rome in AD 210, but Quintus Avadius Rufinus, consul soon after 225, is perhaps more probable, following the discovery of pottery of *c.* 220 in primary levels.

Plate 61

Plate 63

Among other interesting discoveries are parts of three further inscriptions and a piece of an Egyptian granite life-size Imperial statue. No doubt further structural features of the fort and its extra-mural settlement and evidence of its history in the fourth century will be revealed in the excavations still in progress. Material from the fort was used in the construction of the well-known pre-Conquest church within its area and stone from the headquarters building was used in the twin towers of the twelfth-century church, a popular and notable mark from land and sea.

Richborough is the best known of all the forts of the Saxon Shore. RICHBOROUGH It has attracted the attention of antiquaries since Elizabethan days—Camden left the earliest record of an archaeological site defined by crop-marks after seeing the marks of its buildings defined in the growing corn—and it is still among the popular sites of Roman Britain. Excavations started in 1922 by the Society of Antiquaries and continued for sixteen years brought it a wide attention. Something has already been said about the

Figs 53–55
Plate 64

great importance of the site during the Claudian invasion. By about AD 85 it had been levelled off and cleared and a great structure decorated with marble and with life-sized statues in bronze had begun to be erected. It was a monumental four-way entrance-gate to the Province of Britain, the very start of Watling Street and a conspicuous piece of Imperial propaganda dedicated perhaps by Agricola to the Emperor Domitian by whom he was recalled in 84–5. The massive foundations are one of the chief show-pieces of Richborough. Two stone-built house foundations, one a posting-house, remain as visible open-air evidence of an occupation which continued on a military and commercial basis until the middle of the third century. With the advent of barbarian raids from across the North Sea in the third century the great monument was stripped of much of its decoration and converted into an observation or signal tower and defended by a surrounding triple-ditched earthen fort. To this period belongs an inhumation barrow-burial, whose flint superstructure was cut into by the western wall of the Saxon Shore fort, the building which had been started by Carausius before the look-out post had been completed. A pagan temple of the fourth century and a very large number of fourth-century coins point to a long continued occupation which lasted well into the fifth century. Many new details of the site have very recently been published by the Society of Antiquaries of London in the fifth and final Excavation Report edited by Professor Barry Cunliffe.

DOVER

At Dover the walls of the Saxon Shore fort lie beneath the present town and only by chance have odd pieces been seen; the post-war excavations of 1952 revealed nothing of its plan. Its official tiles found in a closed context point to the use of the port by the *Classis Britannica* in the early second to mid-third centuries, and

Plate 65

the importance of the two lighthouses to cross-Channel traffic was paramount. Otherwise there is only the record in the *Notitia* of a garrison of infantry irregulars, the *Milites Tungrecani* of Tongres, who were perhaps moved here by Theodosius.

Lympne is represented by the forlorn walls of Stutfall Castle now some distance from the sea and badly tumbled by landslips. In places they reach 25 feet in height and 14 feet in thickness, with cylindrical bastions and tile bonding-courses. The outline is an irregular pentagon which enclosed about 10 acres. In the *Notitia* its garrison is listed as the *Numerus Turnacensium*, a force of irregular infantry of Tournai which may reflect the events of 369 under Theodosius. Early antiquaries left most readable accounts of the site but even a careful excavation by Roach Smith in the 1840's added little to archaeological knowledge. The principal relic from the fort is a water-worn altar to Neptune dedicated by Aufidius Pantera, prefect of the *Classis Britannica*, which was built into the foundations of the main gateway. There is some reason to think that the altar may have been dedicated in Antonine times; if so, the site where it was originally put up may have been for a while the headquarters of the British Fleet, but Dover with its lighthouses must seem to have pride of place. There is no evidence that Lemanis played any part in the Claudian invasion and coin evidence suggests that the fort was an element in the over-all plan of Carausius. Only a proper excavation, which need not be hurried, can reveal its full story.

Pevensey, again some way from the present-day shore line, lies like Richborough on a small hill above the marshes. Its position is isolated and on the landward side approached only by a minor road from the west. The plan, unlike that of the other forts, is an irregular oval governed by the lie of the land and the 12 foot-thick walls with their ten massive bastions enclose an area of some 8 acres. The 10 foot-wide gates are flanked by towers. Within the Roman walls and in part built on them is the outer bailey and keep of a medieval castle. So far there is no evidence of any early civil settlement or of a Claudian base, though there is a suggestion of occupation in the second century and pieces of *Classis Britannica* tiles. Excavation has revealed the foundation lines of huts presumably for military use. Many late third and early fourth century coins and a coin of 334–5 found under a bastion suggest a possible date for its construction which might coincide with the visit of Constans to Britain. It seems that there was a major reconstruction when Stilicho improved the main defences of Britain; tiles bearing the stamp HON AVG ANDRIA are consistent with this possibility.

Finally we may note that the troubles of the late third and early fourth centuries are also reflected in many hoards of coins, in the burning of farms and villas, and, from a military point of view, in the rebuilding and re fortification of some native hill forts. In Sussex the Caburn, Cissbury and Highdown Hill show evidence of such work.

TOWNS

CANTER
BURY

Canterbury, *Durovernum Cantiacorum*, the cantonal capital of the Cantiaci, grew at the crossing of the River Stour. A Belgic, and indeed an earlier native settlement here have already been noticed in the preceding chapter of this book. The planned programme of excavation in advance of rebuilding on areas damaged by war time bombing has thrown much light on the plan and history of the Roman city which was founded soon after the Claudian invasion. By about AD 270 the walls, the circuit of which was later to be followed by the medieval city walls, enclosed an area of about 130 acres, its streets since Claudian times laid out in a rectangular grid pattern based essentially on the main Dover to London highway. The city was certainly of early growth and its importance and prosperity are indicated by the provision of a forum, the courtyard of which has been located, public baths and sizeable houses at first of clay and half timbering but as early as AD 100 of well laid stone. A small earthen-bank theatre of Romano-Celtic type existed towards the end of the first century; it was rebuilt in classical style and on a surprisingly large scale with a diameter of some 260 feet in the third quarter of the second century. Flour-milling, pottery and tile-making, gravel- and chalk-quarrying in the suburbs outside the walls provided for everyday needs, while imports of wine and the early arrival of workers in mosaic and of sculptors point to the social importance of this, the first stopping-place of all travellers who had landed in the Province of Britain at Richborough or Dover. The settlement was never a military centre, apart from its situation at the focus of roads from the coast, and it seems to have been little concerned with agriculture as an industry, its needs in that direction being supplied perhaps by a large spread of market-gardens. Traces of a jetty, a gravelled causeway and commercial buildings recently excavated in the Westbere Levels at Sturry by Mr Frank Jenkins mark the site of its port. The Stour was navigable here in the second and third centuries and only in Saxon times was this port replaced by Fordwich. A group of four barrows, two just within and the other two just without the walls, is known; the present mound, The Dane John, has one of the barrows incorporated some-where in its structure. The town was still occupied in the fifth century by Romanised Britons who lived side-by-side with Germanic settlers, the federates whom they had invited to aid them in defending the Province.

The Romanised town of Chichester which appears in the CHICHESTER Ravenna Cosmography as a civitas capital, *Noviomagus Regnen-sium*, in all probability succeeded a Belgic settlement at Selsey which with its oppidum and mint has long since been engulfed by the sea. Only the Chichester Dykes, with their deep ditches facing the hill country to the north remain as the probable outer landward defence and boundary of the ancient capital. The new town, on a site occupied by AD 50, covered about 100 acres, a considerably smaller area than Canterbury, and was defined by earthen ramparts before the end of the second century. The early occupa-tion may have been a military one; the grid-pattern of its streets extended beyond the later walls. It was not until the middle of the fourth century, perhaps under the reorganisation of Theo-dosius, that bastions appear to have been added to its walls. The capital of Regnum quickly took an important place in the peaceful Romanisation of the Province and Cogidubnus, ruler of the Regni who remained the faithful ally of the invaders, was set up by them as a client-king owing allegiance to Rome. His name appears as King and Legate of Augustus in Britain, on a very well-known Chichester inscription found in 1723; this dedicates a temple to Neptune and Minerva by the authority of Cogidubnus and a *collegium fabrorum*, a trading guild which like many on the Continent doubtless thrived in the commercial and social atmosphere of Romanisation. After the death of Cogidubnus his regnum was succeeded by the civitas of the Regnenses, its importance marked by the building of a forum and the provision, outside the capital, of an earthern amphi-theatre which, however, never attained a classical dignity. Directly, Chichester may not have seen the volume of official traffic which passed through Canterbury; indirectly, it had experience of most of what mattered in the life of Roman Britain.

ROCHESTER Rochester, *Durobrivae* of the Antonine Itinerary, the Peutinger Table and the Ravenna Cosmography, like Canterbury, was built on or very near to the site of a Belgic oppidum, which apparently possessed its own mint. The main highway of Watling Street here crossed the Medway by a causeway, traces of which were seen many years ago, but almost certainly at an early stage of the occupation a bridge, no traces of which have yet been located, must have spanned the tidal river. The town occupied an area of some $23\frac{1}{2}$ acres. Stretches of the Roman wall still survive, with the medieval city wall following much of its

Plate 67

course. There has been no opportunity for large-scale investigation in the past, but two recent excavations have shown that the Claudian main road was reconstructed no less than seven times and enlarged to form a double carriageway with a central stone-lined gutter, and that between AD 150 and 160 a clay ditch and rampart defence was replaced by a ragstone wall which on the east side of the town still stands to a height of 17 feet. The principal building discovered, a very substantial structure facing the main road, may have been part of the public baths or possibly the forum. There can be little doubt that Rochester was much concerned with the extensive pottery trade of the Lower Medway and with the export of corn and ragstone from the fertile and well-populated Medway Valley, but nothing is known of the nature and situation of its port. A possible example of centuriation near the town has already been noted.

Towards the end of the first century the port of Dover took the place of Richborough as the principal harbour on the south-east coast. Post-war excavations on war-damaged sites and in advance of rebuilding have provided some knowledge to supplement that already existing on the lay-out of the Roman civil settlement, much of which lies under the present town. In the latter part of the second century, the main road to the sea was enlarged to accommodate three lines of traffic, and early in that century a substantial timber quay and jetty were built at the then mouth of the River Dour. Remains of a substantial timber quay were also found in 1885. Official tiles of the *Classis Britannica* suggest the use of the port as the base of a squadron of the Fleet in the second and third centuries. It seems that port facilities may still have been in existence in the fourth century.

The pair of Roman lighthouses, one on each side of the harbour, were associated with the lighthouse built at Boulogne by the Emperor Gaius after his visit in AD 40 in connection with a possible invasion of Britain. That on the western hill, Devil's

Plate 65

Drop, has almost disappeared, but the other on the eastern heights within Dover Castle still stands, though much altered in medieval and later times, as a unique monument of Roman Britain. Its 12 foot-thick walls with bonding courses of tile supported a stepped octagonal tower possibly 80 feet in height. Flame and smoke signals to assist cross-Channel traffic in making the difficult harbour between the tall chalk cliffs could easily have been seen from Boulogne and throughout the passage.

THE COUNTRYSIDE

FISHBOURNE In the countryside of the south-east, indeed in Europe apart from Italy, pride of place must be given to the Palace of Fish-bourne, close to Chichester in Sussex. There was a military occupation of the site in Claudian times as we have already noticed, and little more than thirty years after the invasion there was built a luxurious and exotic classical villa of three wings surrounding a great court with colonnades and covering some $5\frac{1}{2}$ acres. This building, of such an architectural magnificence that it may properly be termed a palace, was in all probability a gift to Cogidubnus the client-king of the Regnenses from his Roman masters. In the Chichester inscription already mentioned he is dignified by the titles of King and Imperial Legate in Britain, and a passage in Tacitus suggests that certain estates were officially bestowed upon him. For the past seven years the site, which was found accidentally by men digging a water-main, has been excavated under the auspices of the Chichester Civic Society and the Sussex Archaeological Society by Professor Barry Cunliffe, and its skilful preservation and the design of its museum are outstanding works in modern archaeology. Much is due to the generosity of Mr Ivan D. Margary and the administration of the Sussex Archaeological Trust. The full history of the building and its final destruction by fire perhaps at the hands of Saxon pirates must be read in Professor Cunliffe's own writings: here it is only possible to mention a few of its outstanding features such as the exceptional mosaics of the second century, the decorative marbles for walls, floors and furniture imported from Tuscany, Skyros and Carrara, the lay-out of the formal garden with bedding-trenches for ornamental flowers and shrubs, indications of fountains and the marble portrait-head of a boy which once stood at one of its corners—all things which everyone at all interested in the Roman Age in Britain should see. No less than 23,000 people did so within the first week of its official opening.

Plate 68

We now turn to the more ordinary buildings of the countryside which exhibit varying degrees of architectural importance but all of which show some evidence of Roman civilised life in their appointments and contents. A few years ago it would have been possible on this broad basis to point to the certain sites of 40 villas, to 20 probable villa sites and to 30 sites of other buildings which ranged from possible villas to rural farmhouses. Very few had been examined with any degree of care and it was nearly always impossible to trace their architectural development and assess, except in a very general way, their function in the economic community. Matters are now greatly improved. Many more sites have been discovered. Much attention is being paid to proper and selective excavation, while as an example of the kind of comparative study which has been so sadly lacking in the past it is possible to cite Mr Brian Philip's survey of agricultural sites in west Kent, a region of mixed farming which in the second century perhaps supported a population of 6,000. A review of the status of the well-known villa at Bignor, Sussex, where the activities on some 2,000 acres of arable, wood and downland were shown by the presence of a barn, ox-byre, cattle-stalls, sheep-pens and a lambing enclosure, is a pointer to the well-organised agricultural background.

To some extent the pattern of distribution reflects the incidence of modern agriculture and commercial development as well as the timely presence of those sufficiently interested in relics of the past to record their discovery. In general the country settlements are sited with access to a road, often on the sheltered side of a hill-slope, and they are found particularly in the valleys of the Medway, Darent, Wey and Mole and along the coastal plain of West Sussex, as well as within easy reach of Watling Street and Stane Street. The number of villas in the valleys of the Medway and Darent suggests a *pagus* based on Rochester; there are relatively few countryside settlements of size around the cantonal capitals at Canterbury and Chichester, but fairly large groups are known on the North Downs Main Trackway in its course through Surrey, around Faversham and Sittingbourne on Watling Street, and near Hardham on the Sussex line of Stane Street.

The southern environs of Londinium, so far as they fall within our definition of the south-east, show a remarkably small settlement of the countryside except at Keston in Kent. The bridgehead at Southwark on the southern bank of the Thames had attractions for countrymen as an urban introduction to the Roman city and this, as well as the possible destruction of evidence in the outward spread of modern London, seems a factor to be borne in mind.

Romanisation inevitably came early to the south-eastern countryside. At Eccles and Farningham there was already wall-painting in the first century and by the end of the century there were baths at Eccles, Angmering and Ashtead, while the first two of these were also provided with wall mosaics in the same century. The villas as a whole exhibit a wide variety of plans, the evolution of which has often remained obscure, and with scant exception it is not known how many were still occupied in AD 410 when Honorius bade the civitates of Britain care for themselves.

At the same time this Romanisation scarcely affected the peasant agriculturists, many of whose primitive settlements amid their fields on the South Downs continued in a native way of life.

Among so many it is impossible here to do more than call brief attention to three villa-sites of outstanding importance which are of more than local interest. Readers especially interested in villas are referred to the comprehensive bibliography in Miss Joan Liversidge's book noted below.

Bignor, in Sussex, already mentioned, has been known since 1811 but not until a re-examination by Professor Sheppard Frere in 1963 was it realised that the stone-built courtyard house was in fact the last of a series of enlargements and rebuildings of a humble timber-framed corridor house first built late in the second century. That the last building fell quickly into decay is clear from the position of its roof-tiles which had fallen on to the collapsed rafters. Columns of Bath stone, walls of good quality Kentish ragstone and imitation marbling were among the notable features of this large but simple building, although it is the very fine fourth-century mosaics which are among the best in Britain that call attention to the taste of its owner, surely a wealthy member of the curial class. Among them the cloaked head of Winter, the surviving member of a Four Seasons pavement, the nimbed head of Venus and a restored frieze of lively cupids dressed as gladiators and acting under the direction of their *lanistae* have a charm rarely to be found.

BIGNOR

The Lullingstone villa on the banks of the Darent was discovered accidentally in the eighteenth century by men putting up a fence; its careful systematic excavation was commenced in 1949 by Col. G. W. Meates and the very fine remains are now preserved by the Ministry of Public Building and Works. On a site once occupied by Celtic farmers a modest but well-built house was erected towards the end of the first century and it contained a deep cellar, then used as a grain store, a Continental feature, which continued to be of importance throughout the history of the villa. The house was enlarged towards the end of

LULLING-
STONE

Fig. 56

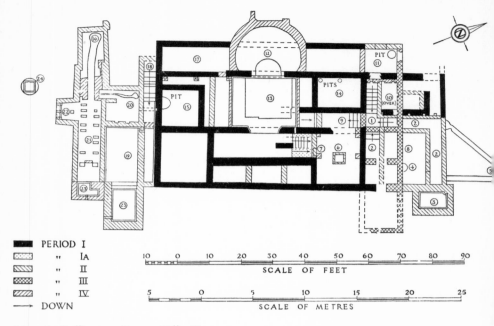

PERIOD I
" IA
" II
" III
" IV
DOWN

SCALE OF FEET

10 0 10 20 30 40 50 60 70 80 90

5 0 5 10 15 20 25

SCALE OF METRES

Fig. 56 Lullingstone Roman Villa, Kent

Plate 70

Plates 71, 72

the second century, given a private bath-suite and a plaster-decorated room for cult worship while the deep cellar was remodelled for the worship of local Water Nymphs, two of whom still survive in a classical fresco painting. It was now a house of distinction, its owner a man of considerable wealth, perhaps a prominent official, who brought with him portrait busts of his ancestors carved in classical fashion in Greek marble and a magnificent gold finger-ring set with a carnelian intaglio of a Winged Victory. As on many other sites in town and country alike, desertion took place and subsequent decay followed early in the third century: it is significant that the owner left his cherished ancestral sculptures to their fate, and that the kitchen of the house became for a short time a tannery. Newcomers took over the site towards the end of the century, making many repairs and enlargements to the house and its baths, removing the portrait busts to the deep cellar room which was now furnished with pots for votive offerings, and building near the river an 80 foot-long ventilated granary. From this time there was a continuous occupation showing wealth and luxury but with some decline towards the end of the early years of the fifth century, when the house was destroyed by fire. This luxury, fully in Roman taste, is well exemplified by splendid mosaic floors in the reception-room and the adjoining apsidal dining-room. The former depicts Bellerophon and the Chimaera with dolphins and the Four Seasons; the latter, the abduction of Europa, is accompanied by a couplet which shows knowledge and appreciation of the Aeneid of Virgil, from which epic also there was a direct quotation on a wall fresco in the Otford villa a few miles away. The Lullingstone villa, centred on its extensive farmlands by the side of a navigable river in an area of smaller houses and villas, lasted with varying degrees of prosperity and fortune for three hundred years. Its remarkable religious associations will be further noted on a later page of this book.

Plate 73

An extensive villa at Eccles, on the east bank of the Medway not far from Rochester, is in course of excavation by Mr A. P. Detsicas. It was built on a palatial scale from the very beginning and its first-century features include mosaics and an elaborate bath-suite with a large circular *laconicum*. Baths were included in the first-century villas at Angmering, Sussex and Ashstead, Surrey, as we have noted, but not on such a magnificent scale. Between 150 and 290 the villa was given the added luxury of a cold plunge bath, large enough to serve as a swimming pool. The signs of an early complete Romanisation in this flourishing agricultural region are clear: one wonders if Eccles was the home of the same sort of family with an official background who later were to build the elaborate barrow-monument at Holborough on the opposite side of the river. Certainly it was an outstanding

ECCLES

feature in the Medway *pagus*. From several points of view this is one of the most important villas in Britain and the further results of its competent investigation are awaited with interest.

INDUSTRY

Few direct traces of animal-rearing on a commercial scale have yet been recorded in the south-east, though some areas on the Sussex Downs bounded by drove-ways may be grazing fields. There is considerable evidence of corn-production: eleven corn-drying kilns were used between about AD 150 and 270 on a small farm at West Blatchington in Hove, Sussex; there were others at Springhead and a large well-ventilated granary was designed to store crops grown in the villa at Lullingstone. Between the rivers Adur and Ouse in Sussex, an area studied in detail by Mr G. A. Holleyman, over 9,000 acres showed evidence of 'Celtic' field-systems and no fewer than thirty-two farming occupation sites. At Thundersbarrow Hill near Shore-ham the wattle huts of a farm-site examined in 1932 by the Brighton and Hove Archaeological Society covered more than an acre; the farm was in use, though not continuously, from the first century until the fourth, at which time corn-drying furnaces were employed to parch wheat before storage. Among a dozen or so other downland farm-sites, all situated on protected sunny slopes, some provide evidence of tiled and glazed houses decorated with coloured wall-plaster and of the Romanised life enjoyed by the peasant farmers. It is probable that small farms existed also on the chalk downs of east Kent, particularly in the Stour Valley, but this region has never been studied in detail as have the South Downs by the long-established school of Sussex archaeologists.

At least two of the countryside establishments were used at some part of their history for the preparation of woollen cloth. Whether this was the cloth of which the *birrus Britannicus*, the rain-cloak listed in the edict of Diocletian, and the *tapete*

Britannicum, the blanket which finds mention in that part of the edict found recently in North Africa, were made can only be a matter of interested speculation. In any event British wool was widely esteemed throughout the Empire, and in addition to its export there must have been a steady home demand. The cleansing and thickening of wool technically known as fulling, and perhaps the subsequent process of dyeing, were almost certainly carried on in a converted villa at Titsey, Surrey, carefully excavated in 1864; the cleansing rooms, the shallow tanks, and a heated room for drying the cloth may still be seen in outline. There is no satisfactory evidence of date, although coin-finds suggest that the conversion to factory premises took place between AD 320 and 340, shortly after which it was burned down. A larger villa at Darenth, Kent, excavated in 1896 and urgently calling for a modern re-examination, was also a flourishing farm later converted by the addition of large heated vats into a fulling and perhaps dyeing establishment. Cement-lined tanks, perhaps part of the equipment of a fulling-mill, have been found within the walls of Chichester.

The mines of the south-east were the principal source of iron for military and civil use and presumably for export. Mining and smelting which was begun in the eastern Weald during the pre-Roman Iron Age was much developed in the second and third centuries. It was worked freely at a dozen or more bloomeries in the Weald, near Faversham in Kent, perhaps experimentally from ironstone in the Forest of Blean between AD 43 and 60, and at the end of the fourth century at Canterbury though the town sites are rather to be associated with urban development than primary smelting-hearths. Unlike other metals, iron does not seem to have been subject to Imperial control, and no administrative centre can be identified. There is however evidence at three of the Sussex Weald bloomeries of some sort of official interest or control. In this way the presence at Bodiam, Bardown and Cranbrook of tiles bearing the stamp of the

Classis Britannica, the British Fleet, can best be explained and it seems possible that the Fleet may have maintained in the Weald a permanent establishment, which included a tile-factory, to serve its needs for iron and ship timber. Iron-slag was freely used as road-metalling, and some idea of the output of the industry may be obtained from the size of the slag-heaps which covered seven acres to a depth of between two and ten feet at Maresfield and two acres in a high tip at Beaufort Park near Hastings.

Among the natural deposits, chalk, Kentish ragstone, the various sandstones of Surrey and Sussex, gravel and clay were worked commercially. Chalk for use in building and for the production of lime must have been quarried on a very large scale, but only two sites have been adequately investigated. A small and much weathered pit at Holborough in the Medway Valley produced sherds of early second-century pottery, and a large quarry on the south side of Canterbury showed the method of deep vertical face working and the access road; at the bottom of the working-face a hoard of at least 108 fourth-century bronze coins had been hidden after the quarry had ceased to be worked. It is clear from its extensive use in forts and town walls, official and domestic buildings and tombs, that ragstone was also quarried on a large scale though no specific Roman workings are known. There can be no doubt that quarries near Maidstone provided much of the stone which found its way widely over south-east Britain, and the wreck of a stone-carrying boat at Blackfriars is an indication of the river route by which it was transported. Gravel for house-flooring, road-making and for use as shipping ballast must have been quarried along most of the river valleys. The enormous quantities used in road-making in Canterbury alone have been the subject of pertinent comment by Mr Frank Jenkins in his account of a Roman gravel pit just outside the town walls. Apart from chalk which is awkward to work for this purpose there is no natural stone in the south-east suitable for carving.

Fig. 57   Ashtead Villa, Surrey. Pattern on tiles

In the well populated south-east there was a great and constant demand for domestic pottery as well as for tiles, and full use was made of a variety of local clays in their manufacture. Among the dozen or so widely distributed pottery kilns and the rather fewer tile-kilns there is nothing like the large-scale organised potters' fields and kiln-yards known elsewhere in Britain. It may be that the industry was to some extent a travelling one, and a centre in the Wey valley close to Farnham in Surrey traded its wares far up into the Thames Valley, though pottery of the kind made in great quantity in the Upchurch area of the Lower Medway was used in east Kent and the coastal fringes but scarcely elsewhere. At Canterbury, in an extensive area of the Medway marshes, and at Bexley and Chalk by Gravesend, careful excavation in recent years has thrown welcome light on both products and kiln-structures, evidence which was sadly lacking in the great collections obtained a generation ago from the Medway marshes. Several of the newly-examined kilns were well in use during Claudian times but on present evidence, which is admittedly insufficient, there seems to be little activity after the second century. One of an interesting series of three kilns at Whitehall, Canterbury, in an area occupied by an extensive cemetery, produced face-urns of a mica-dusted ware; Mr Frank Jenkins suggests that the kiln may have been the property of a funeral furnisher. A solitary mould for Samian ware found at Pulborough, Sussex, is not supported by other evidence of manufacture.

A tile-kiln at Canterbury produced a form of ridge-tile at present not matched elsewhere in Britain; another close to the villa at Eccles was built early in the second century and had a long life. At Plaxtol, Kent, a countryman decorated his box-tiles with his repeated trade-mark which may be extended as *parietalem Cabriabanus fabricavit*, that is, 'Cabriabanus made this wall-tile.' Tiles made in a country factory at Ashtead Common, Surrey, carefully excavated by Mr A. W. G. Lowther from 1925

Fig. 57

onwards, were stamped with lively hound-and-stag hunting scenes, plain chevrons and a conventional zigzag pattern based it is thought on the regimental standards of the auxiliary army. The tiles with animal pattern bore the lettering GIS at the top and at the bottom, upside down, IVFE, an inscription which may perhaps be read as *Gisius fecit*. Products from this factory, which was working from about AD 80 until after the middle of the second century, have been found as far distant as Lincolnshire, Staffordshire and the Mendips, where they were perhaps taken from Ashtead by journeymen tilers.

With two exceptions all the sites here noted are part of the civilian economic scene. Tiles bearing the official stamp of the *Classis Britannica* are well known from Dover and Lympne, which were bases of the Fleet, and they have been noted at a house on the cliff-edge at Folkestone, which with its magnificent seaward view may have been the residence of its British commander, and at Bodiam on the silted-up estuary of the Rother in Sussex, as well as in the Wealden iron-mines and at Boulogne, the headquarters of the Fleet on the Continental coast. Tiles stamped CIB for *Cohors I Baetasiorum*, a known garrison of Reculver, have recently been found within the fort.

To this brief account of home industries there must be added the boiling of salt for food-preservation which was much more extensive than two riverine sites in North Kent would indicate, and the breeding and transport of oysters which, the late Professor Richmond once observed, provided the Romano-British equivalent of modern fish-and-chips. Their empty shells come to light on almost every Roman site in Britain. That they were already in favour in the early part of the second century A D is clear from Juvenal's account of the tastes of Montanus, a sycophant of the Domitianic court, who favoured the oysters of the Rutupine shore.

RELIGIOUS SITES

The posting-station at Springhead, where Watling Street crossed SPRINGHEAD a small tributary of the Thames, has proved to be of much greater importance than even the richly furnished walled cemetery found here in 1799 would have suggested. Since 1950 parts of a 25-acre site were investigated by the late William Penn, and the discovery of a temple area with six temples and another outside the enclosure, a large public bakery with its ovens, a mill and corn-drying kilns, and a series of shops and ancillary buildings point to the existence of what may well be one of the most extensive religious centres yet known in Britain. Here it is not possible to mention more than one or two of its outstanding features.

There is evidence of a Claudian military settlement and a well established road-system. The temple area continued in use with modifications and new buildings from the first century until its partial desecration about A D 370, almost certainly in face of Christian influence though the township seems to have con-tinued its daily life into the fifth century; it was then quietly abandoned, its ruins merging into the flat agricultural landscape, only to be brought to light again in modern times. The temples vary much in size and style. Of particular interest is a magnificent temple of the Romano-Celtic type well known in south-east Plate 75 Britain and northern Gaul but here with an unusual low square tower; it contained a stone altar, a pipe-clay figurine of a goddess, an incense-cup with its contents preserved and votive offerings of a bronze hand and an initial letter, the latter also found else-where on the site, as were offerings of coins fallen from their

193

bags nailed to the plaster walls of corridors. In front of the temple stood a 'Jupiter column' with a Corinthian capital and near by was a tank or pool filled with a mass of broken pots, votive offerings made between AD 150 and 220. A second temple was raised on a podium in classical style, and the entrance to the whole temple area was through a monumental gateway. Such was the religious establishment which with its curious fourteen non-sacrificial infant burials grew around a concourse of eight natural springs, and further excavation will no doubt reveal more of the history of the township and posting-station of which it formed the outstanding feature. Then, too, the significance of a hoard of (at least) 438 silver and three gold fourth-century coins in a pot found accidentally in 1964 may become more clear: the choice of owner at the moment lies between a wealthy inhabitant and an important army or civil officer on his way abroad to follow Magnus Maximus, the commander in Britain who in 383 had revolted and conquered Gaul and Spain.

Springhead is one of the most important sites of its kind in the Province of Britain, but there are several other temples and shrines in the south-east worthy of note. A countryside temple on the slopes of the Downs close to the Kits Coty long barrow at Aylesford recalls the Roman shrine established on Money Mound, the Early Bronze Age barrow in Deer Leap Wood, Surrey already noticed earlier in this book. Temples of the familiar Romano-Celtic type are known on the Downs at Chanctonbury Ring and Lancing Down, Sussex, at Titsey, Surrey close to the well-known villa and at Richborough. Another at Worth not far from Richborough yielded pieces of a statue of Mars or Minerva and two votive shield models from under its foundations, and further welcome evidence of a dedication came from Farley Heath, Surrey—where the foundations of the temple are well preserved—in the form of a bronze sceptre-mounting with representations of the Jupiter-Dispater group of

Fig. 58

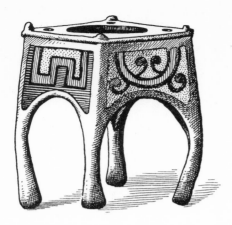

Fig. 58 Farley Heath, Surrey. Above, model stool in enamelled bronze, height 2 ins; right, sceptre-binding, length 9.9 ins

deities, including Sucellos, the Good Striker, who were concerned among their other attributes with a healing cult. A late second-century flagon from Southwark inscribed LONDINI AD FANVM ISIDIS may indicate a temple to the Oriental cult of Isis in the bridgehead settlement on the south bank of the Thames.

At Springhead there was also a devotion to a local goddess who from a clay votive figurine appears to represent a deity not unlike Venus. Native religious cults in Kent, studied for some years by Mr Frank Jenkins, are all associated on the evidence of the clay figurines with fertility, healing and the worship of springs and rivulets. A mother-goddess holding a dog, a god concerned with a horse-cult, a pseudo-Venus and the hooded *genius cucullatus* are all related to their counterparts in Roman Gaul. Eleven small bronze models said to have been found in a barrow in Sussex are related to similar votive objects from the Rhineland, symbols perhaps of Sabazios in an agricultural background.

At the Lullingstone villa Col. G. W. Meates excavated a small circular temple of the early second century, its flint and mortar walls supporting a conical thatched roof. About AD 300 the site was enriched by a temple-mausoleum also on a terrace behind the main house, a tall striking building with a dome of tufa finished in reddish paint. The mausoleum, of Romano-Celtic form, contained the burials of a young man and a young woman in decorated lead coffins enclosed within a substantial timber sarcophagus which was fixed to one wall of the burial-chamber and then battened down with a heavy packing of chalk and gravel. Furnishings for use in the after-life included a bronze and a pottery jug, four fine glass flasks with dolphin handles, two glass bowls, two knives and two spoons, and on the man's coffin, the remains of a gaming-board and a complete set of 30 glass pieces, once contained in a bone-mounted case and accompanied by a medallion of Medusa, which are at present unique in Britain. The burial was robbed in part during the fourth century after the cult-room of the temple built over the mausoleum had fallen into disuse following the adoption of the Christian faith by later occupants of the villa. The interior of the cult-room with its painted red dado and human figures pictured in a pagan ritual against a background of vivid green fully complemented the almost luxurious appearance of its exterior. There can be no doubt of the evidence of Christian faith at Lullingstone. Three rooms of a private oratory with fine wall-paintings of wreathed Chi-Rho monograms and a series of richly-dressed human figures, three at least with arms outstretched in the familiar *orante* pose, all within a richly-coloured pillared portico, remained in use until the building was destroyed by fire in the fifth century. It is the only building of its kind so far discovered in Britain and, most remarkably, it stood over a deeply sunk room in which the pagan worship of ancestors, represented by the two remarkably fine marble portrait busts and libation vessels already noted, continued at the same time as Christian worship in the suite above. Further evidence of Christianity comes from a late fourth- or early fifth-century hoard of Roman gold and silver found in 1962 in Canterbury which includes a spoon and an eating-stick with the Chi-Rho monogram, a useful archaeological confirmation of Bede's words regarding the existence of a Christian community in the Roman city. The treasure also contained a gold ring and a gold hook, two ingots of silver, 10 other silver spoons and a silver pin with a glass head. A cylindrical lead cistern found near Lickfold, Sussex, in 1943 not far from a large villa bears a similar mono-gram and its use as a Christian baptismal font seems at least a possibility.

A so-called temple of Mithras uncovered in 1895 on the banks of the Medway at Burham is nothing more than a storage cellar, probably for corn, of a type found often in Roman Gaul. A similar structure at Chalk by Gravesend, on the Thames, was used as a workshop for the manufacture of bone trinkets at the end of its life late in the third century, and another equally devoid of religious associations is known in North Kent.

For final notice are two marble heads possibly from a shrine to the Imperial cult. From Broadbridge, close to Chichester, comes a finely executed sculpture of Germanicus and from near-by Bosham a large head of an Emperor, possibly Trajan.

FUNERAL MONUMENTS

There are a number of outstanding funeral monuments in the south-east.

Graves, most of them cist-burials with exceptionally rich and elaborate furnishings of a kind frequently found in Gaul, are not uncommon in the Chichester region and alongside Watling Street in Kent. Most of them belong to the late second or early third centuries. Among them a cremation at Aldingbourne, Sussex, accompanied by the frame of a gilded wooden casket and cosmetic in a glass flask, and another at Bayford, Kent, with good glass flagons, bronze oil-flask, lampholder and sacrificial bronzes are worthy of note, as are the number of ornamented lead coffins in North Kent.

Walled cemeteries and funeral monuments within walled enclosures are restricted almost entirely to the south-east; of fourteen known British examples, eight are found in Kent. At Langley and Sutton Valence in the ragstone region there is evidence of funeral pillars which possibly resembled the famous Igel monument near Trier; they may be associated with wealthy families of stone quarriers. A tall mortared flint tower stood within the walls at Borden, Kent. The well-known complex of monuments at Keston, dug at on three previous occasions,

Plate 74

Fig. 59 Holborough Roman barrow, Kent. Model of folding stool. Height of frame 2 ft

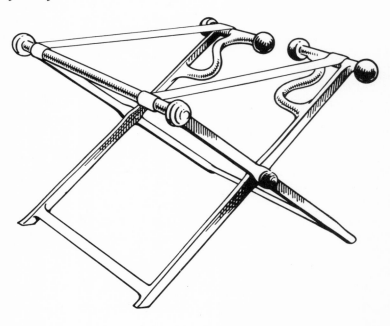

has now been properly excavated by Mr Brian Philp who has conserved the circular mausoleum and found adjoining one of its buttresses a secondary burial in a lead casket contained within a tile-tomb, and 14 other burials, 10 of which were of children, in the immediate vicinity.

A large isolated barrow, Holborough Knob, near Snodland, HOLBOROUGH Kent, excavated in 1954, then one of the only two to have been KNOB examined in Britain for some fifty years, showed many interesting features. Material from an imposing ditch was used to build a small retaining wall; the main burial, by cremation, was in a long shallow wooden coffin placed in a deep grave sunk into the natural chalk and lined with bunches of boxwood, and the funeral ceremony, conducted from a temporary shelter, included the ritual breaking of five *amphorae* of Mediterranean origin and the pouring of a libation of resinated wine. After the ceremony the shelter was burned down and the grave covered with a substantial dome of puddled chalk before the barrow-mound itself was erected. Grave-goods in the main burial and in three shallow pits associated with it, all brought from a cremation pyre elsewhere, included potsherds of the first quarter of the third century, fused glass and burnt bones, a memorial coin to Antoninus Pius depicting a funeral pyre, and the iron frame *Fig. 59* and bronze mountings of a folding stool with remains of the bronze ribbon decoration of its cushion. In the southern part of the mound was a secondary inhumation of an infant with her leather purse and fragments of her fair hair bound with silken damask—the earliest piece yet known in Britain—in a custom-made lead coffin decorated with figures associated with the Plate 69 Dionysiac mysteries, a coffin at present unique in Britain.

Barrows have also been recorded at Canterbury, Richborough, Plaxtol, Stowting and Bishopsbourne in Kent, and in each case the tradition seems to be, as in Belgium and Germany, that of full Romanisation and not Celtic legacy.

L'ENVOI

What of the end of the Roman Age in south-east Britain? The legions had been withdrawn long before the rescript of AD 410 and the official separation meant only a recognition of the complete breakdown of Roman government. The settlement of federates in Kent and the rebellion of 442, both attested by history, may be held to mark the real end. How far Saxon federate troops were disposed on sites of Roman occupation is a matter which is now receiving much attention from archaeo-logists. The discovery of early Germanic pottery in the upper levels of Roman Canterbury, in the ruins of a villa at Wingham in East Kent and in forts of the Saxon Shore may well be significant, as may the discovery of good Roman glass in an Anglo-Frisian cemetery at Hersden not far from Canterbury. In north-east Surrey a group of early Germanic cemeteries in a region of Roman settlement facing London seems also to suggest a degree of continuity or perhaps compromise. With reluctance we must give up our idea that the soldier buried with his gear outside the walls of Richborough was a Saxon pirate, but Mrs Sonia Chadwick Hawkes has shown that previously neglected trifles such as military buckles and belt-fittings can throw light on the darkened passage between Roman Britain and Saxon England.

Sites to Visit

This is a representative selection of field-monuments which are, or were, easily and fairly easily accessible. Monuments on private property are not necessarily open to the public without permission, and some sites on the Sussex Downs in particular have been much altered in appearance by recent ploughing. Those marked * are in the charge of the Ministry of Public Building and Works; those marked † are in the care of the National Trust. The current *List of Ancient Monuments in England and Wales*, H.M. Stationery Office, London, includes all monuments to which State protection has been given. The sections on Kent, Surrey and Sussex in Nicholas Thomas's book *A Guide to Prehistoric England*, London, 1960, can be warmly recommended to the travelling archaeologist.

The area is covered by the following sheets of the Ordnance Survey one-inch map of Great Britain: 169–73, 181–4. Full lists of sites and discoveries are contained in the Indexes to the Period Maps published by the Ordnance Survey:

Ancient Britain, South Sheet, 1964
Southern Britain in the Iron Age, 1962
Roman Britain, 3rd edition, 1956

Kent

PREHISTORIC

Addington, megalithic long-barrow	TQ 653591
Chestnuts megalith	TQ 652592
Aylesford, * Kits Coty megalith	TQ 745608
* Lower (Little) Kits Coty megalith	TQ 744604
White Horse Stone	TQ 753603
Coffin Stone	TQ 739605

Barham Downs, round barrows	TR 208515
Capel, Castle Hill, hill-fort	TQ 607438
Chilham, Julliberrie's Grave, long-barrow	TR 077532
Etchinghill, Brockmans Bushes, round-barrows	TR 160384
Folkestone, Cherry Garden Hill, round-barrow	TR 208379
Harbledown, Bigbury Camp, hill-fort	TR 116576
Iffin Wood, round-barrow	TR 133541
Ightham, † Oldbury Hill, rock-shelters	TQ 585562
† Oldbury Hill, hill-fort	TQ 582561
Lullingstone, Hulberry hill-fort	TQ 518646
Keston (Bromley), Holwood hill-fort	TQ 422639
Keston Common, enclosure	TQ 418642
Nettlestead, Milbays Wood, earthwork	TQ 677508
Ringwould, Free Down, round-barrows	TR 365471
Sevenoaks, Wildernesse, Seal, ? barrow	TQ 538566
Swanscombe, Barnfield pit, site of discovery of	
Swanscombe Man. Nature Conservancy Reserve	TQ 596746
Trottiscliffe, † Coldrum megalithic burial-chamber	TQ 654607
Westerham, Squerryes Park, hill-fort	TQ 443522

ROMAN

Ash, * Richborough amphitheatre	TR 321598
* Richborough Castle, fort	TR 325602
Barham Downs, earthworks	TR 208515
Benenden, paved ford	TQ 802323
Bishopsbourne, Gorsley Wood, barrows	TR 171520
Canterbury, town walls and building in Butchery Lane	
Dover Castle, lighthouse	TR 326418
Folkestone, villa site	TR 241370
Herne Bay, * Reculver fort	TR 227693
Keston (Bromley), tombs	TQ 415634
Lullingstone, * villa	TQ 529651
Lympne, Stutfall Castle, fort	TR 117342
Rochester, town walls	
Stowting, barrow	TR 135424

PREHISTORIC

Abinger Common, Mesolithic pit-dwelling	TQ 112459
Banstead, Tumble Beacon, round-barrow	TQ 243590
Golf Course, round-barrows	TQ 249609
Capel, Anstiebury, hill-fort	TQ 153440
Caterham, Cardinal's Cap, hill-fort	TQ 331532
Chertsey, St Ann's Hill, hill-fort	TQ 026676
Chobham, West End Common, bowl-barrows	SU 931614
Crooksbury Common, triple bell-barrow	SU 893450
Dorking, Milton Heath, round-barrow	TQ 153489
Farnham, Caesar's Camp, hill-fort	SU 825500
Frensham Common, † bowl-barrows	SU 853407
Guildford, Newlands Corner, round-barrow	TQ 045492
Hascombe Hill, hill-fort	TQ 004386
Horsell Common, bell-barrows	TQ 014598
Leatherhead Downs, round-barrow	TQ 182548
Lingfield, Dry Hill, hill-fort	TQ 432417
Puttenham, Golf Course, Frowsbrow, round-barrow	SU 939476
Common, Hillbury, hill-fort	SU 911469
Reigate Heath, round-barrows	TQ 238505
Sanderstead, Addington, round-barrow	TQ 367643
Seale, Crooksbury Common, Soldier's Ring, earthwork	SU 880462
round-barrows	SU 895450
Shere, Holmbury, hill-fort, View-point	TQ 105430
Sunningdale, bowl-barrow	SU 952665
Thursley Common, bowl-barrows	SU 909409
Walton-on-Thames, St George's Hill, hill-fort	TQ 085618
Wimbledon Common, Caesar's Camp, hill-fort	TQ 224711
Wisley Common, bell-barrow	TQ 078592
Worplesden, Whitmoor Common, round-barrow	SU 998536
Wotton, Deerleap Wood, bell-barrow	TQ 118481

ROMAN

Albury, Farley Heath, 'Celtic' temple	TQ 051450
Ashtead, villa	TQ 177601
Compton, villa	SU 958480
Coulsdon, Farthing Down, field-system	TQ 298576, 300577
Titsey Park, villa	TQ 404545

Sussex

PREHISTORIC

Alfriston, Long Burgh, long-barrow	TQ 510034
Angmering, Harrow Hill, flint-mines, hill-fort	TQ 081100
Arlington, Windover Hill, flint-mines, long-barrow,	TQ 545035
round-barrows	TQ 542034
Beddingham, Itford Hill, Bronze Age settlement	TQ 447053
Bignor Hill, † Barkhale causeway enclosure	SU 976126
Brighton, Hollingbury hill-fort	TQ 322078
Whitehawk causeway enclosure	TQ 330048
Black Rock, Nature Conservancy site	TQ 334034
Patcham, Tegdown, round-barrows,	TQ 314101
lynchets	TQ 317098
Chichester Dykes, linear earthworks, *e.g.* SU 860872, 918086, etc.	
Cliffe Hill, long-barrow	TQ 432110
Ditchling Beacon, † hill-fort	TQ 331130
round-barrows	TQ 340128
Dry Hill Camp, hill-fort	TQ 432417
Eastbourne, groups of round-barrows, *e.g.* TV 586987, TV 594984	
Falmer, lynchets	TQ 355113
Ferring, † Highdown hill-fort, Good view-point	TQ 093043
Findon, Church Hill and Tolmere, flint-mines	TQ 112083
Firle Beacon, long-barrow, bowl- and	
round-barrows TQ 486058, 470060–508038	
Charleston Brow, 'Celtic' fields	TQ 484055

Five Lords Burgh, round-barrow	TQ 486036
Frant, High Rocks, hill-fort	TQ 561382
Saxonbury Camp, hill-fort	TQ 577330
Glynde, The Caburn, hill-fort. View-point	TQ 444089
Graffham Downs, round-barrows	SU 915163
Heyshott Downs, round-barrows	SU 895165
Hunter's Burgh, long-barrow	TQ 550036
Jevington, Combe Hill, causeway enclosure	
round-barrows	TQ 574021, 576023
Lewes, platform-barrow	TQ 402110
Oxteddle Bottom, round-barrows	TQ 444104, 446093
Litlington, long-barrow	TQ 535006
Newhaven, Castle Hill, hill-fort	TQ 446000
North Marden, Bevis's Thumb, long-barrow	SU 789155
Old Shoreham, Thundersbarrow Hill, hill-fort, lynchets,	
Iron Age settlement	TQ 229084
Patching, Blackpatch, flint-mines, round-barrows	TQ 094089
Piddinghoe, Money Burgh, long-barrow	TQ 425037
Plumpton Plain, Bronze Age settlement	TQ 358122
Poynings, Devil's Dyke, hill-fort, View-point	TQ 259111
Giant's Grave, round-barrow	TQ 270111
Pyecombe, Wolstonbury, hill-fort	TQ 284138
Rotherfield, Saxonbury, hill-fort	TQ 578330
Seaford Head, round-barrow, hill-fort	TV 495978
Singleton, The Trundle, causeway enclosure and hill-fort,	
View-point	SU 877110
Sompting, Park Brow, Bronze Age settlement, 'Celtic'	
fields	TQ 153086, 153088
South Malling, Ranscombe Camp, hill-fort	TQ 438092
Steyning Downs, round-barrows	TQ 145114
Stoughton Down, long-barrows	SU 823121
Bowhill, Devil's Humps, bowl- and	SU 820111
bell-barrows	SU 807107
Treyford, Devil's Jumps, bell-barrows	SU 825173
Didling-Treyford, barrow with rectangular	
ditch	SU 828177
Waltham Down, bowl- and bell-barrows	SU 929144

Washington, round-barrows, temple-site and Chancton-
        bury Ring, hill-fort, View-point   TQ 139120
West Dean, Goosehill, hill-fort   SU 830127
West Hoathly, Philpotts, hill-fort   TQ 349322
Worthing, † Cissbury, flint-mines, hill-fort,
        View-point   TQ 137079, 139080

ROMAN

Bignor, villa   SU 988148
Bignor-Slindon, † The Gumber, Stane Street road and
        barrows   SU 940105–970128
Chichester, amphitheatre, inscription
Coldwaltham, Hardham posting-station   TQ 030175
Fishbourne, palace
Holtye, excavated road section exposed for inspection
        (Sussex Archaeological Trust)   TQ 461391
Pevensey, * Pevensey Castle, fort   TQ 644048

UNKNOWN AGE

Wilmington, The Long Man, hill-figure   TQ 543095

Principal Museums

(Intending visitors are strongly advised to consult the current annual issue of *Museums & Galleries in Great Britain & Ireland*, Index Publishers, London, for details of opening times, etc.)

London

British Museum, W.C.1
British Museum (Natural History), S.W.7
London Museum, Kensington Palace, W.8
Guildhall Museum, Basinghall Street, E.C.2
Borough of Bexley, Erith, Kent
Borough of Kingston-upon-Thames, Fairfield West
Borough of Southwark, Walworth Road, S.E.17

Kent

Birchington, Powell-Cotton Museum.
Canterbury, Royal Museum
Dartford, Market Street
Dover, Ladywell
Faversham, Maison Dieu, Ospringe
Folkestone, Grace Hill
Herne Bay, High Street
Hythe, Stade Street
Lullingstone, Roman villa
Maidstone, St Faith's Street (and museum of Kent Archaeological Society)
Margate, Victoria Road
Milton-next-Sittingbourne, Court Hall
Richborough Castle
Rochester, Eastgate House
Tunbridge Wells, Civic Centre
Walmer Castle, Gatehouse

Surrey

Camberley, Knoll Road
Godalming, Charterhouse School Museum and Borough Museum, Old Town Hall
Guildford, Castle Arch (and Surrey Archaeological Society)
Haslemere, High Street
Weybridge, Council Offices, Church Street

Sussex

Battle, Langton House
Bexhill, Egerton Park
Bignor, Roman villa
Bognor Regis, Lyon Street
Brighton, Church Street
Chichester, Little London
Hastings, John's Place
Lewes, Barbican House (Sussex Archaeological Society)
Winchelsea, Court Hall
Worthing, Chapel Road

Oxford. The Ashmolean Museum
Cambridge. University Museum of Archaeology and Ethnology
Liverpool. City Museums
Manchester. University Museum
Cardiff. National Museum of Wales, Stopes Collection

Bibliography

Abbreviations

AC   *Archaeologia Cantiana*
AJ   *Archaeological Journal*
Ant.J. *Antiquaries Journal*
Arch   *Archaeologia*
JBAA   *Journal of the British Archaeological Association*
JRS   *Journal of Roman Studies*
PPS   *Proceedings of the Prehistoric Society*
SAC   *Surrey Archaeological Collections*
SxAC   *Sussex Archaeological Collections*

CHAPTER I

BRITISH REGIONAL GEOLOGY: 1960 ed., *The Hampshire Basin*, 1962 ed., *London and the Thames Valley*, 1965 ed., *The Wealden District*.

NEW SERIES SHEET MEMOIRS of the Geological Survey: Chatham, 1954, Maidstone, 1963, Canterbury, 1966. All London, Geological Survey and Museum.

CORNWALL, I. W., 1950, Pleistocene and Holocene sections in deposits of the Lower Thames, *Univ. London Inst. Arch.*, 6th Annual Report, 34.

EVANS, J. H., 1954, Archaeological Horizons in the North Kent Marshes, *AC*, LXVI, 103.

HUME, I. N., 1955, *Treasure in the Thames*, London.

JACKSON, E. D. C. and FLETCHER, SIR ERIC, 1968, Excavations at the Lydd Basilica, 1966, *JBAA*, XXXI, 19.

MARGARY, I. D., 1953, The North Downs Main Trackway, *AJ*, CIX, 39.

SPURRELL, F. C. J., 1885, Early Sites and Embankments on the Margins of the Thames Estuary, *AJ*, XLII, 269.

STEERS, J. A., 1946, *The Coastline of England and Wales*, London.

WOOLDRIDGE S. W., 1932 The Physiographic Evolution of the London Basin, *Geography*, XVII, 99; 1960, The Pleistocene Succession in the London Basin, *Proc. Geol. Assoc.,* LXXI, 113.

WOOLDRIDGE, S. W. and CORNWALL, I. W., 1964, Contributions to a new datum for the prehistory of the Thames Valley, *Univ. London Bull. Inst. Arch.*, IV, 223.

WOOLDRIDGE, S. W. and GOSSLING, F., 1953, *The Weald*, London.

WOOLDRIDGE, S. W. and LINTON, D. L., 1955, *Structure, surface and drainage in south-east England*, London; 1933, The Loam-Terrains of South-East England and their relation to its Early History, *Antiquity*, VII, 297.

ZEUNER, F. E., 1958 ed., *Dating the Past*, London; 1964 ed., *The Pleistocene Period*, London.

Generally, see COPLEY, G. J., 1958, *An Archaeology of South-East England*, London, which covers London and eight counties with parts of three others and contains good distribution maps and a Gazetteer.

Older works are JESSUP, R. F., 1930, *Archaeology of Kent*, London; WHIMSTER, D. C., 1931, *Archaeology of Surrey*, London.

CURWEN, E. C., 1954 ed., *The Archaeology of Sussex*, London, can still be read with profit and delight.

CHAPTER II

CURWEN, E. C., 1954 ed., *The Archaeology of Sussex*, London, Chapters 1 and 2.

DAY, MICHAEL, 1965, *Guide to Fossil Man*, London.

DE VRIES, H. and OAKLEY, K. P., 1959, Radio-carbon dating of Piltdown bone, *Nature*, 184, 224.

OAKLEY, K. P., 1969, Analytical Methods of Dating Bones in BROTHWELL, D. and HIGGS, E. (eds) *Science in Archaeology*, 2nd ed., London; 1964, *Framework for Dating Fossil Man*, London; 1965, *Man the Tool-Maker*, London.

OAKLEY, K. P. and ASHLEY MONTAGU, M. F., 1949, A reconsideration of the Galley Hill Skeleton, *Bull. Brit. Mus. (Nat. Hist.)*, Geology, Vol. 1, No. 2.

OVEY, C. D. (ed.), 1964, The Swanscombe Skull, *Royal Anthrop. Inst. Occasional Paper* No. 20, London.

ROE, D. A., 1964, The British Middle and Lower Palaeolithic, *PPS*, XXX, 245; Gazetteer of British Lower and Middle Palaeolithic sites for Council of British Archaeology.

TESTER, P. J., 1950, Palaeolithic flint implements from the Bowman's Lodge gravel pit, Dartford Heath, *AC*, LXIII, 122; 1953, A Discovery of Acheulian implements in the deposits of the Dartford Heath Terrace, *AC*, LXVI, 72; 1965, An Acheulian site at Cuxton, *AC*, LXXX, 30.

WEINER, J. S., 1955, *The Piltdown Forgery*, London.

WOOLDRIDGE, S. W. and LINTON, D. L., 1955, *op cit.*

WYMER, JOHN, 1969, *Lower Palaeolithic Archaeology in Britain,* London.

ZEUNER, F. E., 1958 ed., *op cit.*; 1964 ed., *op cit.*

CHAPTER III

ALEXANDER, J., 1961, Excavation of the Chestnuts Megalithic Tomb at Addington, Kent, *AC*, LXXVI, 2–3, 29–36.

BURCHELL, J. P. T., 1950, *Nature*, 165, 411 and MS. in Library of Kent Arch. Soc.; for Lower Halstow, 1928, *Proc. Prehist. Soc. E. Anglia*, V, part 3, 289.

CLARK. J. G. D., 1932, *The Mesolithic Age in Britain*, Cambridge; 1936, *The Mesolithic Settlement of Northern Europe*, Cambridge.

CLARK, J. G. D. and RANKINE, W. F., 1939, Excavations at Farnham, Surrey, *PPS*, V, part 1, 61.

CORCORAN, J. X. P. W., 1963, Excavation of the Bell Barrow in Deerleap Wood, Wotton, *SAC*, LX, 1.

FISHER, C. E., 1938, Mesolithic finds at Addington Kent, *AC*, L. 147.

HIGGS, E. S., 1959, Excavation of a late Mesolithic site at Downton . . ., *PPS*, XXV, 209.

KEEF, P. A. M. *et al.*, 1965, A Mesolithic site on Iping Common, Sussex, *PPS*, XXXI, 85.

LACAILLE, A. D., 1961, Mesolithic facies in London and Middlesex, *Trans. London & Mdx. Arch. Soc.*, XX, part 3, 101; 1966, Mesolithic facies in the transpontine fringes, *SAC*, 63, 1.

LEAKEY, L. S. B., 1951, Preliminary excavations of a Mesolithic site at Abinger Common, Surrey, *Surrey Arch. Soc. Research Papers*, No. 3.

MONEY, J. H., 1960, Excavations at High Rocks, Tunbridge Wells 1954–6, *SxAC*, 98, 173; 1962, Supplementary Note, *op, cit.*, 100, 149.

OAKLEY, K. P. *et al.*, 1967, The Skeleton of Halling Man, *AC*, LXXXII, 218.

RANKINE, W. F., 1949, A Mesolithic Survey of the West Surrey Greensand, *Surrey Arch. Soc. Research Papers*, No. 2; 1950, Mesolithic Research in Surrey, *SAC*, LII, 1; 1956, The Mesolithic of Southern England, *op cit.*, No. 4.

SIEVEKING, G. DE G., 1960, Ebbsfleet, *AC*, LXXIV, 192.

CHAPTER IV

ASHBEE, PAUL, 1966, The Fussell's Lodge Long Barrow, *Arch.*, C, 1.

BURCHELL, J. P. T. and PIGGOTT, STUART, 1939, Decorated prehistoric pottery from the bed of the Ebbsfleet, Northfleet, Kent, *Ant. J.*, XIX, 405.

BRUCE-MITFORD, R. L. S., 1938, A hoard of Neolithic axes from Peaslake, Surrey, *Ant.J.*, XVIII, 279.

CLARK, GRAHAME and PIGGOTT, STUART, 1933, The Age of the British Flint Mines, *Antiquity*, VII, 166; 1965, *Prehistoric Societies*, London.

CLARK, J. G. D., 1952, *Prehistoric Europe*, Cambridge; 1966, The Invasion Hypothesis in British Archaeology, *Antiquity*, XL, 172.

CURWEN, E. C., 1954 ed., *The Archaeology of Sussex*, London, Chapters V and VI.

DUNNING, G. C., 1966, Neolithic Occupation sites in East Kent, *Ant.J.*, XLVI, 1.

EVENS, E. D. *et al.*, 1962, Fourth Report ... on the Petrological Identification of Stone Axes, *PPS*, XXVIII, 209.

GREENFIELD, E., 1960, A Neolithic pit ... Wingham, East Kent, *AC*, LXXIV, 58.

JESSUP, R. F., 1937, Excavations at Julliberrie's Grave, Chilham, *Ant.J.*, XVII, 122; 1939, do *Ant.J.*, XIX, 260.

OAKLEY, K. P. *et al.*, 1939, *A Survey of the prehistory of the Farnham District*, Surrey Arch. Soc., Guildford.

PAYNE, G., 1880, Celtic remains discovered at Grovehurst, Milton, *AC*, XIII, 122.

PIGGOTT, STUART, 1954, *The Neolithic Cultures of the British Isles*, Cambridge; 1965, *Ancient Europe*, Edinburgh.

PIGGOTT, STUART and KEILLER, A., 1939, The Badshot Long Barrow in Oakley *et al.*, 1939.

SMITH, ISOBEL F., 1965, *Windmill Hill and Avebury, Excavations by A. Keiller 1925–39*, Oxford.

SMITH, W. CAMPBELL, 1963, Jade Axes from . . . the British Isles, *PPS*, XXIX, 133.

WOOD, E. S., 1950, Neolithic sites in West Surrey, *SAC*, LII, 11.

CHAPTER V

ALEXANDER, J., 1961, Excavation of the Chestnuts Megalithic Tomb, Addington, Kent, *AC*, LXXVI, 1.

BENNETT, F. J., 1907, *Ightham, the story of a Kentish village*, London; 1913, Excavations at Coldrum, Kent, *Journ. Royal Anthrop. Inst.*, XLIII, 79.

CRAWFORD, O. G. S., 1924, The Long Barrows and Megaliths . . . Sheet 12 of the ¼-inch map, *Ordnance Survey Professional Papers*, N.S. No. 8, Southampton.

DANIEL, G. E., 1950, *The Prehistoric Chamber Tombs of England and Wales*, Cambridge; 1958, *The Megalith Builders of Western Europe*, London, subsequently 1963 in Penguin Books, Harmondsworth; 1967, Northmen and Southmen, *Antiquity*, XLI, 313.

EVANS, J. H., 1948, Smythe's Megalith, *AC*, LXI, 135; 1950, Kentish Megalith Types, *AC*, LXIII, 63; 1952, The Tomb of Horsa, *AC*, LXV, 101.

FILKINS, E. W., 1928, Excavations at Coldrum, Kent, *Ant.J.*, VIII, 356.

McCRERIE, ALAN, 1956, Kits Coty, Smythe's Megalith, the General's Tombstone, *AC*, LXX, 250.

PIGGOTT, STUART, 1954, *op cit*.

RENFREW, COLIN, 1967, Colonialism and Megalithismus, *Antiquity*, XLI, 276.

Victoria County History, Kent, 1908, Vol. 1, 317.

CHAPTER VI

ASHBEE, PAUL and DUNNING, G. C., 1960, The Round Barrows of East Kent, *AC*, LXXIV, 48.

BALDWIN, R. A. and KELLY, D. B., 1966, Walderslade, *AC*, LXXX, 285.

BECKENSHALL, S. G., 1967, Excavation of Money Mound, *SxAC*, 105, 13.

BURSTOW, G. P., 1958, Late Bronze Age Urnfield on Steyning Round Hill, Sussex, *PPS*, XXIV, 158.

BURSTOW, G. P. and HOLLEYMAN, G. A., 1958, Late Bronze Age Settlement on Itford Hill, Sussex, *PPS*, XXIII, 167.

CLARKE, D. L., 1962, Matrix Analysis and Archaeology with particular reference to British Beaker Pottery, *PPS*, XXVIII, 371; 1968, *The British Beaker Culture and its Regional and Chronological Subcultures*, Cambridge.

CURWEN, E. C., 1954, *The Archaeology of Sussex,* Chapters VII–VIII, London.

GORDON, M. S., 1966, Gold Bracelets from Little Chart, *AC*, LXXX, 200.

HOLLEYMAN, G. A. and CURWEN, E. C., 1935, Late Bronze Age lynchet-settlements on Plumpton Plain, Sussex, *PPS*, for 1935, 16.

HAWKES, C. F. C., 1935, Pottery from sites on Plumpton Plain, *PPS* for 1935, 39; 1942, The Deverel Urn and the Picardy Pin . . ., *PPS*, VIII, 26, but see SMITH, M. A., 1959.

LONGWORTH, I. H., 1961, The Origins and Development of the Primary Series in the Collared Urn Tradition . . ., *PPS*, XXVII, 263.

MEGAW, B. R. S. and HARDY, E. M., 1938, British Decorated Axes and their Diffusion, *PPS*, IV, 272.

MUSSON, R. C., 1954, An Illustrated Catalogue of Sussex Beaker and Bronze Age Pottery, *SxAC*, 92, 106.

PARSONS, JOHN, 1962, Broomwood Bronze Age Settlement, *AC*, LXXVI, 134.

PIGGOTT, C. M., 1949, A Late Bronze Age Hoard from Blackrock in Sussex . . ., *PPS*, XV, 107, but see SMITH, M. A., 1959.

POWELL-COTTON, P. H. G. and PINFOLD, G. F., 1940, The Beck Find (Birchington, Kent), *AC*, LI, 191.

SMITH, M. A., 1959, Some Somerset Hoards and their place in the Bronze Age of Southern Britain, *PPS*, XXV, 144 (see also SMITH, ISOBEL, 1961, *Helenium*, I, 112, and BUTLER, J. J., 1956, *Palaeohistoria*, 5, 75).

WOOD, E. S. and THOMPSON, N. P., 1966, A Food Vessel from Abinger Hammer, Surrey, *SAC*, 63, 44.

WORSFOLD, F. H., 1943, Late Bronze Age site at Minnis Bay, Birchington, Kent, 1938–40, *PPS*, IX, 28.

The following hoards are illustrated and described in detail on the cards of *Inventaria Archaeologica*, Great Britain Series, now published by the British Museum.

G.B.18   Harty, Kent, 3rd set, 1956, ed. M. A. Smith.
G.B.37   Worthing, Sussex, 6th set, 1958, ed. M. A. Smith.
G.B.40   Beachy Head, Sussex, *op cit*.
G.B.47   Blackrock, Sussex, 7th set, 1959, ed. M. A. Smith.
G.B.48   Ramsgate, Kent, 8th set, 1960, ed. D. Britten.
G.B.53   Bexley Heath, Kent, *op cit*.
G.B.54   Addington, Surrey, *op cit*.

CHAPTER VII

ALLEN, D. F., 1944, The Belgic Dynasties of Britain and their coins, *Arch.*, XC, 1; 1955, Three Ancient British Coins (Vodenos), *Brit. Num. Journ.*, XXVII, 249; 1958, Belgic Coins as Illustrations of Life in the late pre-Roman Iron Age of Britain, *PPS*, XXIV, 43; 1961, The Origins of Coinage in Britain, in Frere, 1961; 1962, Celtic Coins in *Ordnance Survey Map of Southern Britain in the Iron Age*.

APPLEBAUM, S., 1955, The Agriculture of the British Early Iron Age, *PPS* for 1954, XX, 103.

ARTHUR, J. R. B., 1954, Prehistoric Wheats in Sussex, *SxAC*, 92, 37.

BIRCHALL, ANN, 1965, The Aylesford-Swarling Culture; the Problem of the Belgae reconsidered, *PPS*, XXXI, 241.

BOYDEN, J. R., 1958, Excavations at Hammer Wood, Iping, *SxAC*, 96, 149.

COTTON, M. A. and RICHARDSON, K. M., 1941, A Belgic Cremation Site at Stone, Kent, *PPS*, VII, 134.

CUNLIFFE, B., 1966, Stoke Clump, Hollingbury and the early pre-Roman Iron Age in Sussex, *SxAC*, 104, 109.

CURWEN, E. C., 1954, *The Archaeology of Sussex*, 2nd ed., London, Chapter IX.

DETSICAS, A. P., 1966, An Iron Age and Romano-British site at Stone Castle Quarry, Greenhithe, *AC*, LXXXI, 136.

FRERE, S. S., 1942, An Iron Age site near Epsom, *Ant.J.*, XXII, 123; 1944, An Iron Age site at West Clandon, Surrey, and some Aspects of Iron Age and Romano-British Culture in the Wealden Area, *AJ*, CI, 50; 1961, (Ed) Problems of the Iron Age in Southern Britain, *Univ. London Inst. Arch., Occasional Papers* No. 11; 1967, *Britannia, a History of Roman Britain*, London, Chapters 1 and 2.

HASTINGS, F. A., 1965, Excavation of an Iron Age Farmstead at Hawk's Hill, Leatherhead, *SAC*, LXII, 1.

HAWKES, C. F. C., 1959, The ABC of the British Iron Age, *Antiquity*, XXXIII, 170; 1961, do in Frere, 1961; 1968, New Thoughts on the Belgae, *Antiquity*, XLII, 6.

HELBAEK, H., 1952, Early crops in Southern Britain, *PPS*, XVIII, 194.

HODSON, F. R., 1962, Some pottery from Eastbourne, the 'Marnians' and the pre-Roman Iron Age in Southern England, *PPS*, XXVIII, 140; 1964, Cultural Groupings within the British pre-Roman Iron Age, *PPS*, XXX, 99.

JENKINS, F., 1962, *Men of Kent before the Romans, Canterbury Arch. Soc. Occasional Papers* No. 3, Canterbury.

JOPE, E. M., 1961, Daggers of the Early Iron Age in Britain, *PPS*, XXVII, 307.

KEEF, P. M. A., 1950, Harting Hill Hut Shelters, *SxAC*, 89, 179.

LOWTHER, A. W. G., 1946, Excavations . . . Queen Mary's Hospital, Carshalton, Surrey, *SAC*, XLIX, 56.

MARGARY, I. D., 1952, The North Downs Main Trackway, *AJ*, CIX, 39.

POWELL, T. G. E., 1958, *The Celts*, London.

RADFORD, C. A. R., 1955, The Tribes of Southern Britain, *PPS*, XX, 1.

RIVET, A. L. F., 1962, *The Ordnance Survey Map of Southern Britain in the Iron Age*, Chessington, Surrey; 1964, *Town and Country in Roman Britain,* 2nd ed., London, chapter 2.

WARD PERKINS, J. B., 1938, Early Iron Age site at Crayford, Kent, *PPS*, IV, 151; 1944, Excavations on the Iron Age Hill-fort of Oldbury, *Arch.*, XC, 127.

WILSON, A. E., 1955, Sussex on the eve of the Roman Conquest, *SxAC*, 93, 59.

WILSON, A. E. and BURSTOW, G. P., 1948, The Evolution of Sussex Iron Age Pottery, *SxAC*, 87, 77.

CHAPTER VIII

BURN, A. R., 1953, The Battle of the Medway, A D 43, *History*, 39, 105.

CUNLIFFE, B. W., 1962, Excavations at Fishbourne, *Ant.J.*, XLII, 15; 1963, *Ant.J.*, XLIII, 1; 1964, *Ant.J.*, XLIV, 1; 1965, Fish-bourne, 1961–4, *Antiquity*, XXXIX, 177; 1968, Fifth Report . . . Richborough, Kent, *Reports Research Com. Soc. Ant. Lond.*, XXIII.

CURWEN, E. C., 1954 ed., *The Archaeology of Sussex, London*, Chapter 10.

DETSICAS, A. P., 1963– , Excavations at Eccles, *Arch. Cant.*, LXXVIII, 125 and vols for 1964–7 continuing.

FRERE, S. S., 1962 ed., *Roman Canterbury*, Canterbury Arch. Soc., Canterbury; 1963, Bignor Roman Villa, *JRS*, LIII, 155; 1967, *Britannia, a History of Roman Britain*, London.

HAWKES, S. C. and DUNNING, G. C., 1961, Soldiers and Settlers in Britain, Fourth to Fifth Century, *Medieval Arch.*, V, 1.

HOLLEYMAN, G., 1935, Celtic Field Systems in South Britain, *Antiquity*, IX, 443.

GOODCHILD, R. G., 1947, The Farley Heath Sceptre, *Ant.J.*, XXVII, 83.

JENKINS, FRANK, 1966, *Roman Kent, Canterbury Arch. Soc. Occasional Papers* No. 5, Canterbury.

JESSUP, R. F., 1954, Excavation of a Roman barrow at Holborough, *AC*, LXVIII, 1; 1958, Barrows and Walled Cemeteries in Roman Britain, *JBAA*, XXII, 1; 1962, Roman Barrows in Britain, *Coll. Latomus,* LVIII, 853, Brussels.

KENYON, K., 1959, Excavations in Southwark, *Surrey Arch. Soc. Research Papers* No. 5, Guildford.

LIVERSIDGE, JOAN, 1968, *Britain in the Roman Empire*, London.

LOWTHER, A. W. G., 1947, Excavations at Ewell, *SAC*, L, 9; 1954, do *SAC*, LIII, 27.

MARGARY, I. D., 1965 ed., *Roman Ways in the Weald*, London; 1967, *Roman Roads in Britain,* London.

MEATES, G. W., 1955, *Lullingstone Roman Villa*, London; 1962, *Lullingstone Roman Villa*, Min. Public Building and Works Guidebook; official excavation report in course.

NIGHTINGALE, M. D., 1953, A Roman Land Settlement near Rochester, *AC*, LXV, 150.

PAINTER, K. S., 1965, A Roman Silver Treasure from Canterbury, *JBAA*, XXVIII, 1; 1965, A Roman Marble Head from Sussex, *Ant.J.,* XLV, 178.

PENN, W. S., 1952, Excavations at Springhead, *AC*, LXV, 171 and vols for 1958–67 continuing.

PHILP, BRIAN, 1966, *The Roman Fort at Reculver*, Reculver Excavation Group, Herne Bay, Kent; 1968, *Excavations at Faversham, 1965*, First Research Report, Kent Arch. Research Groups' Council, Bromley, Kent; 1968, Excavation of the Roman Cemetery at Keston, *Kent Arch. Review*, No. 11, 10; No. 12, 15, Bromley.

RICHMOND, I. A., 1961, A new Building Inscription from ... Reculver, *Ant.J.,* XLI, 224; 1965, do. *JRS*, LV, 220.

RIVET, A. L. F., 1964 ed., *Town and Country in Roman Britain*, London.

WACHER, J. S., 1964, Survey of Romano-British Town Defences of the early and middle Second Century, *AJ*,CXIX, 103.

WACHER, J. S. (*Ed.*), 1966, *The Civitas Capitals of Roman Britain*, Leicester University Press.

WEBSTER, G. and DUDLEY, D. R., 1965, *The Roman Conquest of Britain,* London.

WHITE, D. A., 1961, *Litus Saxonicum*, Madison, Wis.

WILSON, A. E., 1952, Chichester Excavations, *SxAC*, XC, 164; 1956, The Beginnings of Roman Chichester, *SxAC*, XCIV, 100; 1962, Chichester, *SxAC*, C, 73.

WINBOLT, S. E., and HERBERT, G., 1965 ed., *The Roman Villa at Bignor,* Chichester.

Victoria County History, Surrey, IV, 1912; Kent, III, 1932; Sussex, III, 1935.

Sources of Illustrations

PLATES

Photographs specially taken by Mr Brian J. Philp; Plates 22–24, 26, 27, 29, 61, 63, 74. The air photographs, Plates 11, 12, 35, 44, 45, 62. Air Ministry, London and University of Cambridge Committee for Aerial Photography (photographs by Dr J. K. S. St Joseph, Crown Copyright reserved). Plate 1: Aerofilms Ltd. Plates 2–5, 14 are from Geological Survey photographs, Crown Copyright, reproduced by permission of the Controller, H.M. Stationery Office. Plates 30, 64–66, 70, 73 are reproduced by the courtesy of the Ancient Monuments Department of the Ministry of Public Building and Works, Crown Copyright reserved. Plates 15—17, 31, 36, 38—41, 54, 57—59 are by courtesy of the Trustees of the British Museum, British Museum Copyright. Plate 6 is from the British Museum (Natural History) Copyright. Plates 8–10, 51, 52 are by courtesy of the London Museum, London Museum Copyright; Plate 53 Guildhall Museum; Plates 49–50 Manchester University Museum; Plates 13, 18, 32 Brighton Art Gallery and Museum; Plates 33, 47, 48, 56, 69 Maidstone Museum; Plate 42 Royal Museum, Canterbury (photograph W. L. Entwistle); Plates 71, 72 by the courtesy of Lt. Col. G. W. Meates and the Kent County Council (British Museum photographs); Plate 7 the late Mr W. S. Penn and the Kent Archaeological Society (photograph Mr P. A. Connolly). Plate 28 is by the courtesy of Dr John Alexander; Plate 60 by Connold, East Grinstead; Plate 68 Professor B. W. Cunliffe (photograph Mr David Baker); Plate 43 Mr Frank Jenkins; Plate 7 Mr J. M. Money (photograph *Kent & Sussex Courrier*); Plate 37 Mr Edwin Smith; Plate 67 Dr Francis W. Steer; Plate 34 Mr E. S. Wood (photograph Mr Thomas Wilkie) and Plates 46 and 55 (photograph Mr Ivor Morgan) Kent Archaeological Society. Plates 19–21 and 25 are by the Author.

FIGURES

The maps Figs. 1 and 30 are by Mr H. A. Shelley; Figs. 8, 26–29 by Mr C. O. Waterhouse, M.B.E. Figs. 2, 3 and 58 are reproduced by the courtesy of the Trustees of the British Museum; Figs. 22–25 and 52–55, the Society of Antiquaries of London; Figs. 6 and 7 Royal Anthropological Institute; Fig. 49 Royal Archaeological Institute; Figs. 45 and 48 Kent Archaeological Society; Figs. 9, 33, 34 Dr John Alexander and the Kent Archaeological Society; Figs. 35–36 Mr J. H. Evans and the Kent Archaeological Society; Fig. 5 Mr P. J. Tester and the Kent Archaeological Society; Fig. 56 Lt. Col. G. W. Meates and the Ministry of Public Building and Works; Figs. 42 and 43 Messrs G. P. Burstow and G. A. Holleyman and the Prehistoric Society; Figs. 11 and 12 Professor Grahame Clark and the Prehistoric Society. Fig. 4 is by the courtesy of Mr J. Bernard Calkin; Fig. 51 by Mr N. C. Cook; Fig. 37 Mr G. C. Dunning; Fig. 39 Mrs Margaret Guido; Fig. 57 Mr A. W. G. Lowther; Figs. 13 and 14 Professor Stuart Piggott and Fig. 18 after the late J. H. Pull.

The Author is particularly grateful to the Sussex Archaeological Society which with its customary courtesy has given facilities for the use of many drawings from the Curwen Collection, most of them the work of that talented artist Robert Gurd. They include Figs. 10, 15–17, 19–21, 38, 40, 41, 44, 46, 47 and 50. Messrs Methuen & Co. Ltd have kindly raised no objection to the use of illustrations which appeared in Dr E. Cecil Curwen's book *The Archaeology of Sussex*, 1954 edition.

6

7

8

9

10

11

12

13

14

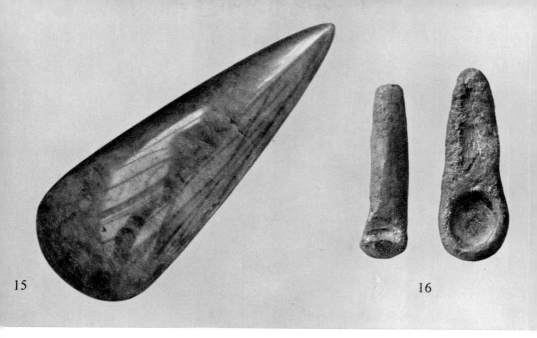

15   16

17   18

19

20

21

22

23

24

25

26

27

28

29

30

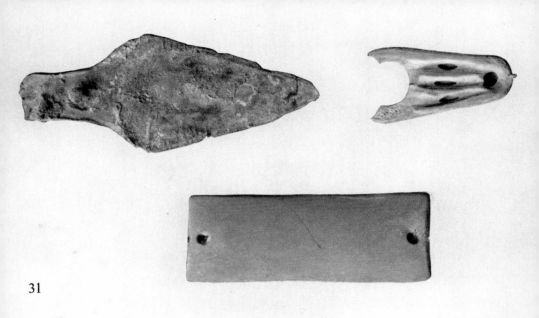

31

32

33

34

36

37

38

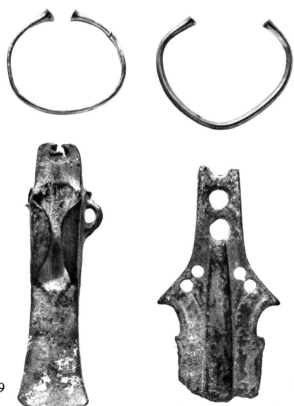

39

40

41

42

43

44

45

46

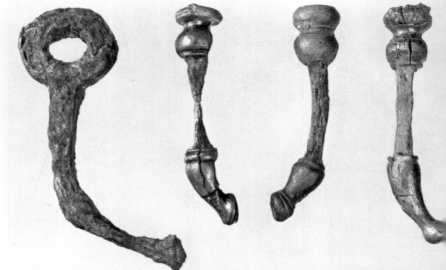

47

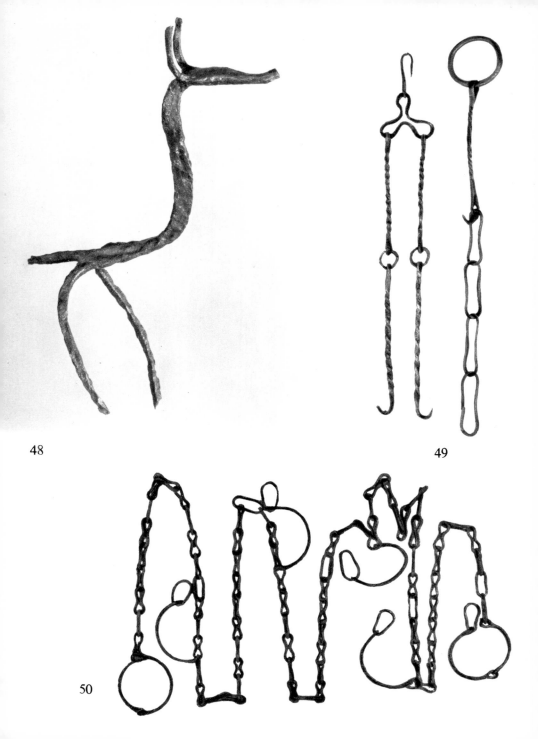

48

49

50

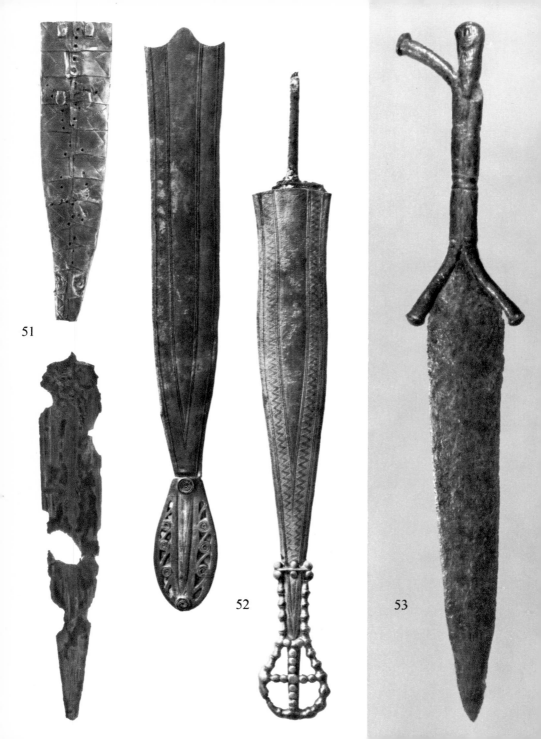

51

52

53

54　　55

56

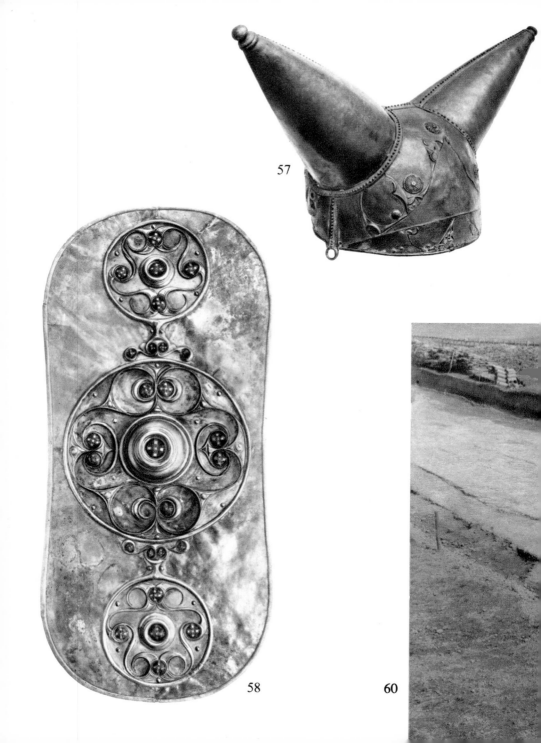

57

58

60

59

61

62

63

64

65

66

67

68

69

71

72

73

74

75

Notes on the Plates

1 The Sussex Downland: Devil's Dyke, an aerial view of the pre-Roman Iron Age promontory fort from the north-east looking across downland to the sea.

2 The Medway Gap in the North Downs from a point behind Wouldham between Rochester and Maidstone, a photograph taken before modern building spoiled the landscape. The line of a branch of the North Downs Trackway, here known as the Pilgrim's Way, is clear along the base of the hills in its course towards Rochester. The valley was widely settled from early prehistoric times onwards into the days of established history.

3 The Greensand escarpment in Surrey overlooking the Weald; a view looking eastward from Gibbet Hill near Hindhead. In the centre distance is Hascombe Hill with its Iron Age promonotory fort and far distant, on the left, Leith Hill (965 ft O.D.) the highest point in the south-east.

4 The Sussex coast at Blackrock, Brighton. A thick deposit of Coombe Rock overlies a raised pebble beach which in turn rests on undisturbed chalk. The raised beach was laid down when the sea-level was 20–30 feet higher than it is today. The 60-foot deposit of Coombe Rock belongs to a succeeding period of extreme cold; it contains much angular flint, blocks of Wealden sandstone and sarsen, and has guttered down over an old sea-cliff cut in the chalk at the time the raised beach was being formed. The site is notified as of special scientific interest under Section 23 of the National Parks Act, 1949.

5 Oldbury Hill, Ightham, Kent: a natural pent-house in the green chert of the Folkestone Beds which almost certainly served as a rock-shelter

in Mousterian times. A large collection of flint implements, mostly of Mousterian character, was excavated about 1890 from trenches in the hill-side below.

6   The Swanscombe skull, vertical view. The bones are undistorted and the sutures open. Three parietal depressions are visible, one, on the left parietal, perhaps the result of a slight injury. The condition of the sutures suggests death at an age in the early 20's and the individual was probably a female. Maximum breadth 142 mm. Cranial capacity 1325 cc. British Museum (Natural History).

7   High Rocks, Tunbridge Wells, Kent/Sussex. The overhang, no doubt a rock-shelter, on Site F with excavation work in progress on the hearths and scatter of flints and pottery. The occupation lies about 4 feet below the present surface level. It was from this site that material for radio-carbon dating was taken.

8   Lower parts of barbed antler points, probably fish-spears, of Magle-mosean form dredged from the Thames. *Top:* Battersea, London, length 8.2 in. *Below:* Wandsworth, London, length 5.5 in. London Museum.

9   Upper part of plain bone point made from tibia of red deer, grooved and narrowed for attachment to shaft. Dredged from the Thames at Battersea, London. Length 8 in. London Museum.

10 Mattock-head with circular perforation and bevelled edge made from antler of red deer. Found in marsh clay 15 feet below the surface, Bankside, Southwark, London. Length 7.75 in. London Museum.

11 The Iron Age hill-fort, Cissbury, Sussex, from the north. The site has been described by Mr T. G. E. Powell as a classical example of the bivallate contour hill-fort dating probably from the mid-third century B C. The filled-in shafts of Neolithic-Bronze Age flint-mines are clearly

visible as are the lynchets of native and Roman cultivations. One of the two original entrances may be seen on the left-hand side: that in the foreground is modern. The square enclosures within the major earth-works are probably to be connected with the refortification towards the end of the Roman occupation.

12 Harrow Hill near Angmering, Sussex. This view from the air shows the filled-in shafts of a large group of flint-mines and a small rectangular hill-fort or cattle-compound of the Iron Age. The ramparts of the enclosure cover and cut through the shafts of the flint-mines.

13 Antler pick and shovel made from the shoulder-blade of an ox: flint-mines at Cissbury, Sussex. The pick is 6.6 in. long. Brighton Art Gallery and Museum.

14 Flint-mine at Blackpatch Hill, Patching, Sussex, showing three of eight radial headings at a depth of 10 feet from the surface.

15 Polished jadeite axe with straight sides converging towards the pointed butt and thin pointed oval section: it is probably an import from Brittany. Found at Canterbury in circumstances not recorded. Length 8.5 in. British Museum.

16 Two clay spoons from Hassocks, Sussex. One account says that they were scratched out of the side of a disused sand-pit by rabbits, another, by the same author, that they came from a rectangular grave covered with a softly-baked tile. Length of the larger 4.5 in. British Museum. A third example now in Maidstone Museum was found many years ago near Ightham, Kent. Such spoons have been attributed to the Windmill Hill culture in Britain.

17 A classical specimen of 'Mortlake Ware' of the Secondary Neolithic, a heavy round-based bowl with prominent shoulder and thickened rim. The decoration is by whipped cord and finger-nail impressions.

Dredged from the Thames at Mortlake, Surrey, with pieces of similar pottery and fragments of a beaker. Diameter 6.8 in. British Museum.

18 Two bowls reconstructed from sherds excavated at Whitehawk cause-wayed enclosure near Brighton, Sussex. They are of good quality ware and exhibit the lugs and rim-forms characteristic of this type of pottery. Diameter of larger 5.1 in. Brighton Art Gallery and Museum.

19 Bevis's or Baverse's Thumb, a Sussex long-barrow near Up Marden. It is 210 feet long, 60 feet wide and 6 feet in height at this, the east, end.

20, 21 Julliberrie's Grave, Chilham, Kent, before excavation in 1937. This is an isolated unchambered long barrow with a surrounding ditch which was still partly open in Roman times. The views are of the western side and the southern end where it is 42 feet in width. The site is now much overgrown and impossible to photograph satisfactorily. This ia a re-photographed illustration: the original negative, prints and block were destroyed during the war.

22 Kit's Coty House, Aylesford, Kent: the remaining trilithon and cap-stone. The left-hand trilithon stands 8 feet in height above ground.

23 The Upper White Horse Stone, Aylesford, Kent: probably the remain-ing stone of a megalithic burial chamber; there is no trace of a mound.

24 Lower Kit's Coty or the Countless Stones, Aylesford, Kent. The site has recently been fenced by the Ministry of Public Building and Works. No trace of the mound is now visible.

25 Coldrum, Trottiscliffe, Kent: the burial-chamber looking west from the top of the mound.

26 Coldrum, Trottiscliffe, Kent: the burial-chamber from the east. Fallen stones from the peristalith lie at the foot of the natural terrace.

27 The Chestnuts megalithic tomb, Stony Warren, Addington, Kent, after excavation and restoration. View from the forecourt.

28 Chestnuts megalithic tomb: a façade stone is being pulled to a vertical position after excavation in 1957.

29 Addington, Kent: the north-east area of the long barrow with stones of the peristalith. The site is now much overgrown and difficult to interpret.

30 Beakers from East Kent in Walmer Castle Museum. *Left:* Sholden Bank, Upper Deal, found with a crouched burial in a grave just over 5 feet deep in the chalk. Height 8.75 in. *Right:* St Margaret's-at-Cliffe, a well-made and finely decorated pot found with a human skeleton in a shallow grave in the chalk. A flint arrow-head and a stone hammer are said to have been found with it. Height 4.75 in.

31 Riveted bronze knife, bone belt-hook and bowman's wristguard of grey slate, length 3.75 in., from an inhumation burial in a cist-grave dug 5 feet deep into the natural chalk. The knife was by the left arm. Sittingbourne, Kent, found in 1883. British Museum.

32 The Hove barrow: perforated whetstone, length 2.5 in.; cup carved from a block of amber, height 2.5 in.; perforated stone battle-axe, length 4.7 in.; bronze dagger with rivets for handle and traces of leather-lined scabbard, length 5.5 in. Brighton Art Gallery and Museum.

33 Two of the pots from the western barrow, Free Down, Ringwould, Kent. The globular urn with twisted cord and chevron pattern, height 3.5 in., was found standing on the incense cup, height 2.25 in., which is perforated with two holes near the base and was said to contain a burnt substance resembling linen. Faience beads and an urn with applied 'horseshoe' decoration provide further evidence of a connection with the Wessex culture. Maidstone Museum.

34 Abinger Hammer, Surrey: food-vessel of southern type generally associated with the early part of the Wessex Bronze Age culture. Nothing was found with it. Height 4.5 in. Guildford Museum.

35 Kingley Vale near Stoughton, Sussex: air view from the south of a group of Wessex-type barrows. A small farmstead site, lynchets and a boundary ditch all probably of the same period lie close by.

36 Cauldron of riveted bronze plates with reeded looped handles set inside rim. Late Bronze Age. Diameter 22.5 in. Dredged from the Thames near Battersea, London. British Museum.

37 Three Sussex or Brighton bronze loops found in a merchant's hoard at Blackrock, Brighton, Sussex, with palstaves, a dirk and a dirk-handle, a spiral ring and two armlets. Over-all diameter of left-hand loop 3.5 in. Brighton Art Gallery and Museum.

38 Part of a Late Bronze Age hoard of more than 190 pieces which include looped palstaves, winged axes, looped and socketed axes, carp's-tongue swords, a socketed knife, a hog-backed knife, tanged sickle, plain socketed spear-heads and three tubular toggles which suggest a connec-tion with horse-gear of the Hallstatt culture. Ebbsfleet, Minster-in-Thanet, Kent, where the owner had probably just landed. British Museum.

39 Part of a hoard found at Beachy Head, Sussex, in 1806 after a landslide: two of four gold penannular bracelets, a winged axe and the hilt of a carp's-tongue sword. Length of winged axe 5.25 in. British Museum.

40 Gold penannular bracelets, Dargets Wood, Walderslade, Kent, found without any associations in 1965. The plain bracelet of Armstrong's type 3 has hollow trumpet terminals; maximum diameter 3.2 in. The solid ribbon bracelet is decorated with 12 double concentric circles set

within double engraved lines and its terminals are sharply everted. Maximum diameter 2.8 in. Late Bronze Age. British Museum.

41 Massive gold torc, ribbed, coiled, twisted and with plain ends. Found at a depth of 6 feet at Castle Mount, Dover, Kent, 1878. Weight 12 oz. Late Bronze Age. British Museum.

42 Unique silver coin of Vosenos (Vodenos) found in excavations near the Marlowe Theatre, Canterbury, in 1953. It is of bright white silver, slightly cup-shaped and very finely struck; weight 17.7 gr., maximum diameter 0.6 in. The reverse here illustrated has a horse walking right and the legend in diagonal retrograde. The coin is 'typical of a Celtic artist's restless treatment of his subjects . . . in offering three irreconcilable view points'. It can be dated in the first ten years of the first century AD before the district of Kent was infused with the classical influence so noticeable on the coins of Eppillus. See Allen, D. F., 1955, where the coin is published in full detail with interesting comments on its technique. Canterbury Museum.

43 Canterbury: stake-holes of the Early Iron Age. A settlement under the junction of Castle Street and St John's Lane excavated in 1946.

44 Mount Caburn, Beddingham, Sussex: air view from the east. The granary pits of the earlier settlement are clearly visible in the interior, and the massive rampart and wide ditch of the later re-fortification appear on the right.

45 The Trundle, Singleton, Sussex: air view from the north showing the bold ramparts and ditch of the Iron Age hill-fort and the Neolithic causewayed-enclosure within the interior.

46 Oldbury, Ightham, Kent: the Iron Age hill-fort, part of the north-east gate and the adjacent rampart showing the lip of the earlier ditch which

has been deliberately filled in by the builders of the later defences. The figure on the right stands on the post-hole of the later gate.

47 Bronze-mounted iron linch-pins, Bigbury hill-fort, Harbledown, Kent. Length of largest 4.5 in. Maidstone Museum.

48 Iron fire-dog, Bigbury hill-fort, Harbledown, Kent. This, the most interesting piece of metal-work in a large collection from the site, is badly rusted and though it cannot be compared with other well-known fire-dogs from Britain and the Continent, the sensitive treatment of the snuffling muzzle is worthy of note. The piece is small, height 10.75 in., and although there are records of iron tyres from the site it is much more likely to have been a fire-dog than a chariot-mounting. Maidstone Museum.

49 Iron pot-hangers, Bigbury hill-fort, the largest 45 in. long. That on the right is an example of Professor Piggott's 'Common Market' products. Manchester University Museum.

50 Iron gang-chain, Bigbury hill-fort, length 18 feet. Manchester University Museum. (It should be noted that all the material from Bigbury came from casual gravel digging in the mid-nineteenth century: see Jessup, R. F., 1933, Bigbury Camp, *Arch. Journ.*, LXXXIX, 87.)

51 Iron dagger and bronze-bound sheath, Hallstatt D type, from the ballast of the Thames, Mortlake, Surrey; length 10.5 in. Fragments of the sheath, perhaps of birch bark, remain on the blade. The sheath had a pair of iron suspension loops, the rust impressions of which can be seen on the blade. London Museum.

52 *Left:* bronze dagger-sheath of La Tène I type from the Thames at Hammersmith, London, length 11.5 in. The bone or ivory handle is said to have been thrown away by the finder. The oval chape is decorated with open-work scrolls and punched dots. British Museum. *Right:*

bronze and iron dagger-sheath of La Tène I type from the bed of the Thames, Richmond, Surrey, length 12.75 in. The bronze front plate is decorated with incised chevrons and dots and a notable feature is the H-pattern and a circle above it most carefully executed. The knob-ornamented chape is cast in one piece of bronze. British Museum.

53 Iron dagger from the Thames at Southwark, London, length 13.75 in. The anthropoid hilt is a single tube-forging. Guildhall Museum.

54 Detail of handle attachment of bronze-mounted wooden bucket from the Aylesford, Kent, Belgic cemetery. It contained cremated bones and was in Dr Birchall's burial group Y with Italian bronzes, a brooch, a pedestal urn and three open-mouthed jars. The bucket has a diameter of 10.5 in. British Museum.

55 Bronze mount for a bucket handle, Boughton Aluph, Kent. Found in a clod of mud on the wheel of a tractor when it had been stabled after a day's ploughing. The highly stylized Celtic human mask with its horns suggests a representation of the Gaulish stag-antlered god Cernunnos. The eyes were probably inlaid with enamel though no trace remains. Height 6.5 in. Kent Archaeological Society's Collection, Maidstone Museum.

56 Group, probably a hoard, of gold staters from near Ryarsh, Kent. The first in the top row is of Gallo-Belgic C type, the others of Gallo-Belgic E. Twice natural size. Maidstone Museum.

57 Bronze horned parade helmet from the Thames at Waterloo Bridge, London. Width between tips 16.75 in. The scored roundels appear to have been set with red enamel. It is usually dated in the first century BC. British Museum.

58 Bronze shield, perhaps originally gilded, dredged from the Thames at Battersea, London. Length 2 ft 6.5 in. This is one of the finest pieces

of mature La Tène art from Britain. The scroll and palmette decoration is enriched by ornamental studs set with red glass, each stud being fastened into the shield by a central pin. This parade object is usually dated to the first century B C or in the early years of the first century A D. British Museum.

59 Part of a hoard of 34 Roman *aurei* found at Bredgar near Sittingbourne, Kent, in 1957. The coins show progressive wear according to age. Left to right, chronologically, are *aurei* of the Republic, Tiberius and Claudius. The latest issue in the hoard was an *aureus* of Claudius of A D 41. British Museum.

60 The London–Lewes Roman road with the original iron-slag surface and its wheel-ruts exposed by excavation at Holtye near East Grinstead. Part is preserved by the Sussex Archaeological Trust and open to view.

61 Reculver, Kent: a section of the first bath-house east of the church excavated in 1965 by the Reculver Excavation Group. This third-century building originally with a vaulted roof and brightly-painted interior walls was robbed extensively for the construction of the pre-Conquest church.

62 Reculver, Kent: air view from the west. The walls of the Saxon Shore Fort are visible at the top and side of the picture where they follow the line of the hedge on the right. The pre-Conquest church and the later twin towers—the Sisters of Reculver in legend—lie near the cliff edge. The area at the top of the picture was formerly an oyster-bed. The place has altered much since this photograph was taken.

63 Fragments of an inscription found during recent excavations in the ruined strong-room of the Headquarters building of the Saxon Shore fort at Reculver. It may thus be reconstructed:

AEDEM PRINCIPIORVM
CVM BASILICA
SVB A TRIARIO RVFINO
COS
) FORTVNATVS
) T

That is:

> For the Emperor . . . Fortunatus built this shrine of the Headquarters
> with the cross-hall under Aulus Triarius Rufinus consular governor.

64 Richborough Castle, Kent. This air view shows clearly the walls of
the Saxon Shore fort and its outer ditches, the third-century triple
ditches surrounding the foundations of the great monumental arch,
Watling Street leading from the arch out by the west gate and, between
the triple ditch fort and the walls of the Saxon Shore fort, a sector of the
ditch of the Claudian camp. The River Stour runs in the foreground,
and the site of the Roman harbour lies off the picture to the bottom
right-hand.

65 The Roman pharos at the west end of the church of St Mary-in-Castro,
Dover, Kent. It may have served as a second axial tower to the pre-
Conquest church. The tower, square within and octagonal without,
stands to a present height of some 40 feet but was originally much taller.

66 Pevensey Castle, Sussex. Air view from the north-west showing the
wall of the Saxon Shore fort with its gateways and bastions, and the
inner medieval castle.

67 The Cogidubnus inscription found in 1723 close to a Roman building
which may have been a temple in North Street, Chichester, Sussex.
It dedicates a temple to Neptune and Minerva by authority of Cogidubnus and a guild of artificers. The stone is Purbeck marble. It may be
seen in a glazed case in the portico of Council House in North Street.
The restored inscription would read:

NEPTVNO ET MINERVAE
TEMPLVM
PRO SALVETE DOMVS DIVINAE
EX AVCTORITATE TI CLAVD
COGIDVBNI REGIS LEGATI AVGVSTI IN BRITANNIA
COLLEGIVM FABRORVM ET QVI IN EO
SVNT DE SVO DANT DONANTE AREAM
(CLE)MENTE PVDENTINI FILIO

That is:

To Neptune and Minerva this temple is dedicated for the safety of the Imperial Family by the authority of Tiberius Claudius Cogidubnus King and Imperial Legate in Britain by the guild of artificers and its associated members from their own contributions the site being given by (Cle)mens son of Pudentius.

68 Fishbourne Roman palace near Chichester, Sussex. A general view across the garden looking west showing the bedding trenches for the hedges which flanked the north side of the central path. The diagonal ditches crossing the excavation trench are modern field-drains.

69 Lid of lead coffin from the secondary burial in a Roman barrow at Holborough, Snodland, Kent. It contained the skeleton of a one-year-old child who had a leather purse and a head-band of silk damask, the earliest yet found in Britain. The Maenad, Satyr and baby Satyr are figures from the world of the Bacchic mysteries derived perhaps from an eastern Mediterranean copy-book. Second or third century AD. Length 3 feet 6 in. Maidstone Museum.

70 Lullingstone Roman villa, Kent. Restored second-century wall-painting of water nymphs from the deep cult-room.

71 Lullingstone Roman villa, Kent. Portrait bust of a man by a Mediterranean sculptor in Greek marble. The style is characteristic of the

Hadrianic and early-to-mid Antonine periods. Found with No 72 in the deep room accompanied by a votive pot.

72 Portrait bust of a man in Greek marble with its pedestal broken in antiquity, found with No 71. The style is rather later, perhaps *c.* 155–165, and the bust might represent the owner of the villa, a man in the imperial service, or a member of his family.

73 Mosaic pavements in the Lullingstone Roman villa. This is the Europa panel with its inscription in the foreground, and the panel depicting Bellerophon and the Chimaera bounded by the Four Seasons may be seen in the room beyond. Fourth century. The Europa panel is 8 feet in width.

74 Keston, Kent. Restored Roman mausoleum and adjacent tomb-chamber after recent re-excavation during the course of which many new burials including a cremation placed in a lead canister within a tile-tomb were discovered. The monument is now in the care of the Greater London Borough of Bromley.

75 Romano-Celtic Temple I, Springhead, Kent. This air view from the south-east shows the entrance porch with flanking wings and mosaic, the destroyed mosaics of the vestibule, the cella with its apsidal suggestus and altar-site and the projecting Roman strong-room. It is perhaps the best preserved temple of its kind in Britain.

Index

Index